the

GAME
& the
glory

the

GAME

& the

glory

by Michelle Akers

with Gregg Lewis

Zonderkidz
The Children's Group of Zondervan Publishing House

jb
AKERS

CONTENTS

 Introduction
While the World
Looks On

The Women's World Cup was clearly THE biggest sports story in the summer of '99. Never before in America had soccer been so celebrated. Never before in sports history had a women's team attracted so much attention as the U.S. Women's National Team. Never before in human history had a team of female athletes become such sudden worldwide celebrities.

Here's just a small sampling of the World Cup media glare Michelle Akers and her teammates experienced.

JUNE 15
San Francisco Chronicle

In February, FIFA president Sepp Blatter declared that "the future of football is feminine."

Well, the future is now.

Beginning Saturday ... at various stadiums around the United States, the 16 best female soccer teams from around the globe will be contending for their sport's highest honor, the Women's World Cup. . . .

JUNE 24
The Los Angeles Times

The war horse is being readied for battle once again. The attendants have done what they can to patch her up and prepare her physically and mentally. They have buckled on the armor and wished her luck. There is little more they can do.

Another tournament is underway and she is going out, as she has every year since 1985, to take on the world and show why she still is the finest, the most respected and certainly the most courageous women's soccer player of her generation.

[Michelle Akers] is ready. . . .

JULY 5
San Diego Union Tribune

Akers has meant everything to the U.S. women's soccer team from the beginning. She was Mia Hamm before Mia Hamm. Before anyone cared about the women's team. She scored the very first goal. She scored two goals in the victorious final of the inaugural Women's World Cup in 1991. With 104 career goals, she is only one of four women on the planet to reach the century mark.

She's not the team's most prolific scorer anymore, but she proved again yesterday how valuable she can be. Her teammates call her Mufasa, after the proud father in *The Lion King,* because of her mane of brown curls. . . .

The Seattle Times

Michelle Akers looked as if she'd been mugged.

She had taken a boot in the face from Brazilian striker Sissi. She had been kicked in the head—the result of another vicious tackle by Tania. There was a knot on the back of her head and an ache in her right shoulder.

"You couldn't have pulled her out of that game with wild horses," Keeper Brianna Scurry said. "She was staying in there. You would have had to cut her leg off to get her out. She's a role model for everybody on this team. Whenever I get a little tired, I think of Michelle. I see her still pushing and that makes me keep pushing."

Akers won balls in the air. She won balls at her feet.

She cleared a dangerous ball intended for Sissi in the 35th minute when the Brazilians were attacking in tsunamis.

Her flick to Mia Hamm set up the run that resulted in a penalty inside the box.

And Akers' resulting penalty kick blurred past keeper Maravilha in the 80th minute, giving the U.S. the security goal it needed.

"You're my hero," Hamm told her as they walked off the field.

The New York Daily News

"It's a privilege to be her coach," U.S. coach Tony Di-Cicco said. "There has been no other woman who has played the game to her level.... She is a champion...."

Before Mia Hamm, Akers was the first women's soccer superstar.... Her prolific scoring pace once was a goal per game....

But in [the early 90's], she suddenly developed chronic fatigue syndrome. She had no energy. She couldn't walk, let alone run. She tried diets, various programs, and turned to religion. She is a devout Christian, which has helped her get through it.

"I wasn't thinking, 'Why me, why me? Poor Michelle,'" Akers said. "It was more, 'What does this mean? How do you want me to change?' That was the question I would shout at God."

JULY 10
The New York Times

No one could be disappointed by the way Michelle Akers has played in this tournament, and while some of her teammates now get more attention, not one has been more vital to the American success in reaching [the] championship match against China in the Rose Bowl. Akers, the first great star of this team ... is [now] the oldest player on the team, and perhaps the most indispensable.

"She's the best woman that's ever played the game, period," said Tony DiCicco, the American coach.

Chapter One
Who Will I Be?

I awakened before 5 A.M. as usual, alone in the quiet darkness of my hotel room. This was the morning of July 10, the day of the 1999 Women's World Cup soccer final.

Of course I knew about all the media attention the World Cup tournament had generated around the world. In the past few weeks I'd talked to more reporters for more interviews than I could count. But I hadn't been reading the papers or watching TV.

Of course I realized the significance of playing in the final game at the Rose Bowl in front of ninety thousand people with a worldwide television audience tuned in. Getting another shot at a world championship had been a major focus of my life and that of my teammates ever since the '95 World Cup and the '96 Olympics.

Certainly this promised to be a big day.

But I still needed to begin the morning with my usual daily routine.

Like every morning of my life in the eight years since I'd developed Chronic Fatigue Immune Dysfunction Syndrome (CFIDS), I did a mental check. I needed to know, *How am I feeling today?*

I definitely had a sense of tiredness—enough that I could tell I wouldn't know until I got on the field and started warming up just how much gas I had left in my tank. *No sense worrying about that now.*

Sitting up in bed, I began my usual daily quiet time of Bible study and prayer. That done, I pulled out my personal World Cup journal, and at the top of the page I wrote:

7/10—Game Day vs. China—The World Cup Final

I'm not sure what to think or what exactly I'm feeling prior to this game. I have a strange sense of destiny, of call. It's like the calm before a battle, I suppose. All the preparation is behind me. Now it's finally time.

Nothing to do now but show up, be courageous, give everything, and see what happens.

Before the Brazil game last Sunday, I stood in front of the mirror and looked into my own eyes to try to see into myself. I noticed the black shadow still around my eye from my broken face back in February. I wondered, *Would I have the courage required to meet this challenge?* I looked even deeper into myself and asked how different I would be after the game. I came home from that game against Brazil having fought a valiant battle.

Another guts game for me. But I had what it took and I hadn't flinched or hesitated.

Today I peer into my eyes and ask the same questions of courage and destiny. But now I also see a cleat mark and a bruise on my face alongside the remaining black eye.

When I stopped writing to think about it, I realized why I felt so beat up. Game after game throughout the tournament, something new had happened to me physically. And I knew from experience it was gonna happen again. I was already weary and sick and beat up. And I had another 90 minutes to go today—with the entire world watching.

During the whole year leading up to the World Cup and now all during the tournament as well, I'd sensed God was doing something very important in my heart and life. But growth never comes without a price.

Sometimes it seemed like I'd been running this marathon obstacle course forever. Every game, every day was like one more hurdle, one more test placed in my path. I'd faced so many challenges, expended so much of my energy reserves, and endured so much pain that some days I wanted to scream out at God, "That's enough! I can't go on!"

But when I did go on, I realized God was strengthening me, changing me, one day at a time. I was slowly learning I didn't have to worry about whether or not I could overcome the obstacles, whether or not I succeeded in reaching my goals, or even whether I ever crossed the finish line. All that God expected of me was to be faithful. To take the next step. That would be enough because He would make it enough.

I just knew I had to be steadfast—to step up and step out one day at a time. *Will I be able to do that for one more game? What will happen if I do?* In my mind those were the crucial questions that made this the biggest game of my life.

With that realization I finished my journal entry:

> Who will I be when I return to this room and look into the mirror after today's game? I don't know. But I think the key is that I'm willing to put myself on the line to find out.
>
> Joshua 1:9—"Have I not commanded you? Be strong and courageous. Do not be terrified; do not be discouraged, for the LORD your God will be with you wherever you go."
>
> Here I go!

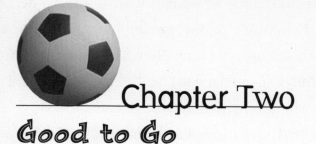

Chapter Two

Good to Go

After a breakfast of oatmeal, and a team meeting, I packed my game gear. That done, I met one-on-one—as we usually do on game days—with Coach Tony DiCicco to talk about my assignment for the game.

I understood my role very well. As "holding midfielder" my primary offensive assignment was playmaker, the quarterback of the offense. My job was to control the ball in the middle, to change the point of attack from one side of the field to the other, to get everyone else involved, and to pass the ball ahead for my teammates.

On the attack, if we had a chance to press an advantage, I could move up, launch an outside shot anytime I got a chance, try to get my head on the ball in the box, and maybe even get a rebound near the top of the penalty box.

But the thing Tony emphasized most was my defensive role. In addition to dominating the midfield, I had one other challenge: stopping China's leading striker, Sun Wen. So Tony expected me to know where she was and to track her whenever she came into my area.

That would be one tough assignment. The Chinese are very skillful and fast all over the field. Their main strength is possessing the ball, which forces opponents to spend a lot of time and energy chasing. If we let them play their usual game, it could be exhausting. And one of the more serious side effects of my CFIDS is that when I get especially tired, I no longer think quickly or clearly.

I get what they term "shocky"—my body starts going into shock, the blood goes to my vital organs instead of into my arms and legs. As my blood pressure drops, the blood flow to my brain diminishes, my mind gets mushy, and I lose concentration. A tornado roars in my head, my thoughts scatter, and my body feels weighted down and slow as molasses. Sometimes I've actually gotten delirious on the field and had to be led to the bench by my teammates or the trainers.

I can't afford that this afternoon. If I'm tracking Sun Wen, I gotta be on. One half-second of distraction or a single mistake in judgment could cost a goal, or the game and a world championship.

"How are you feeling today?" Tony asked as we concluded our meeting.

"I'm good to go!" I tried to assure him with a smile. But I knew that Tony knew that I couldn't be sure of anything until I got out on the field to see how my body responded.

Arriving at the Rose Bowl after a short bus ride, we unloaded our gear and tried to make ourselves at home in the locker room as we prepared for the game.

Brandi Chastain and I had developed a little World Cup '99 tradition of our own. Once I get all my gear on, I have a meaningful Bible verse and the name of a person to whom I want to dedicate that game written on my sock tape just below my shinguards. At the opening game of the tournament at Giants Stadium I'd asked Brandi to write my personal inspirational message of the day on my socks for me. She'd done it every game since, always remembering to come over and ask me, "Who's this game for, Mish? What's the verse today?"

For the final, it wasn't the name of one person, just the Bible reference I'd recorded in my journal that morning. So Brandi took a permanent marker and wrote "Josh 1:9" on each sock. Then she used my camera to take a photo of her handiwork for my World Cup scrapbook.

Shortly after the reserves left to go out to the field, the starters headed out into the tunnel leading onto the field. There the American and the Chinese teams assembled in single-file, parallel lines against opposite walls of the corridor to await the ceremonial procession into the stadium.

Moments later the music began to play and the two teams marched side by side to midfield for the playing of national anthems. When all ninety thousand screaming fans stood to acknowledge our arrival, I feared I'd never locate my dad for our usual pregame salute.

Shielding my eyes against the glare of the overhead sun, I finally saw the signs held by a long row of family and friends—one big bold letter per placard. It was at least halfway up the stands, but I could make out the message: "Pig Farmer—#10." I had to laugh—it was an old family joke. I pointed at Pops and gave him a big thumbs up. I couldn't see his face clearly from that distance, but I knew he was grinning back, and his very presence made the game all the more special. Throughout my soccer career, my father's encouragement has always meant more than anyone else's. And I knew I needed that encouragement today.

We stood at attention at midfield as the national anthem played and a squadron of jets roared overhead. During the introductions, Mia Hamm reached over and slapped my shinguards—our longtime tradition. I remember thinking, *This is it! The very last World Cup game of my career!* I wanted to soak it all in: the crowd, the anthem, the look on the Chinese faces, Mia and Julie Foudy standing on either side of me, our bench cheering us on, everything.

I remember telling myself, *You've got 90 minutes left. It's time to blow it out. Gotta score early and then hold the lead.*

Play. Score. Win. Go home. That was my personal game strategy.

With temperatures climbing into the nineties and field temperature well over a hundred, I felt near exhaustion soon after the start of the game. *At this rate,* I told myself, *I'm not gonna last to the half.*

The pace was too frantic. As usual, the Chinese attack was intense. I was dying. It was as if my reserve tank had sprung a serious leak; I could feel what energy I had left steadily draining out onto the turf.

If I'm going to make a difference, I need to do it NOW. I began pressing forward hoping to get a chance to score, so we could get a goal, relax, hold the lead, and go home World Cup champs. That's why I moved up when, in just the 8th minute of the game, the referee called a Chinese foul and awarded us a free kick from the left side some forty yards out. The moment Mia Hamm's right foot made contact with the ball I sprinted into the box. No one picked me up. As Mia's shot bent toward the back post I stretched out in a feet-first slide to try to redirect on goal. My lunging right foot actually contacted the ball in the air just a few yards out. But I couldn't control it. My deflection sailed harmlessly to the right of the goal, over the end line.

I raced back into position for the goal kick thinking, *If only I'd been a half step quicker!*

Then in the 12th minute, I stole the ball in midfield, dribbled past one opponent, ran past another, and saw my next shot. At thirty-five yards I'd created the slightest of openings and took a half chance—blasting a long attempt that the Chinese goalkeeper gathered in for her first save of the day.

For the remainder of the first half, my chances to score were few and far between. I withdrew into my playmaking position, won as many headballs as I could, marked and tracked my girl Sun Wen, and watched the clock tick down to halftime.

☺ ☺ ☺

Neither casual fans nor the most expert observers could tell just how much Michelle was struggling. Indeed, ABC's television broadcasters repeatedly noted her effort—on this day and throughout the World Cup. When she just missed the deflection/shot in the 8th minute, play-by-play announcer J.P. Dellacamera exclaimed, "What a warrior Michelle Akers is for this U.S. team. She's had too many injuries to mention. Yet she's been their best field player in this tournament."

Color commentator Wendy Gebauer agreed, calling her "the most consistent player for the U.S. She's the heart and soul of the midfield as well. Her performances have been amazing."

A few minutes later, Gebauer referred to her as someone "who has done more for this sport than any player in the world."

Due to a stifling U.S. defense, the Chinese got off only two shots the entire first half—neither of those on goal. Michelle's primary assignment, Sun Wen, seldom even touched the ball.

In the 38th minute, Michelle broke up China's most serious (and perhaps only real) threat when she sprinted into the goal box and dove past a Chinese player to head a loose ball over the end line and out of play. But that effort sent her sprawling to the turf again, sliding and crashing into the advertising signs at the end of the field.

"Michelle never holds back," Gebauer commented.

Her broadcast partner added, "She plays every game like it's her last."

✿ ✿ ✿

I wondered for a while if that first half was going to be my last.

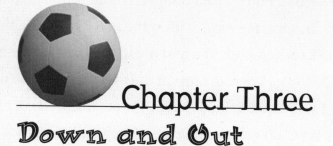

Chapter Three
Down and Out

By the time we got to the locker room, I hurt so bad I felt as if I were going to die. I have no idea what Tony and the other coaches told the team in their half-time talk. I had collapsed on the floor in the back of the locker room with a cold wet towel wrapped around my neck and shoulders. With the help of the team trainer I refortified myself with a couple granola bars, some Gatorade, and as much coffee as I could stomach to try to raise my blood pressure.

I will play till I drop. Just 45 more minutes, I told myself. *I'll play minute by minute if I have to—until I have nothing left.*

Putting on my best game face, I walked out to my position to start the second half—fighting to find that last bit of reserve I knew I could find if only I reached deep enough. *Lord, help me be strong and courageous!* I prayed.

The second half started out even more physical than the first. In separate plays within the first 2 minutes, the Chinese knocked both Mia and me to the ground in violent collisions. I knew the rest of the way was going to be rough. I was also terrified that as I tired, one of the Chinese girls would get loose for a half step and score.

I quickly determined that as long as I could stay on my feet, my personal goal was to own the midfield and win every ball on the ground and in the air. Anybody in my area who wanted the ball was going to pay.

Ever since I came down with CFIDS in 1991, I've noticed three crucial times in almost every game I play. It's like I hit a wall 15 to 20 minutes into the first half. If I can make it through that, I seem to catch a second wind. But halftime is always another bear. It seems once I've stopped moving, it takes a superhuman effort just to get going again. When I can start the second half, I often actually begin to feel a little stronger, until I hit another, seemingly bigger, wall, right around the 70-minute mark.

When that happens, it's like a hole opens up in the bottom of my soul. As the last of my strength drains out, I feel myself slipping away until I'm empty, just a shell, with nothing but guts inside.

So anytime I manage to last until the final minutes of any game, I'm pretty much a zombie on the field. My teammates watch me carefully. When they see my eyes glaze over, Lil (Kristine Lilly), Julie Foudy, or team captain Carla Overbeck will literally get right in my face and yell at me, "Mish, stay in there! We need you!"

The only way I can describe the sensation is to say it's like trying to play in a dark tunnel. All I can see or focus on is whatever is right in front of me—*if* I can just manage to really, really concentrate.

I was playing all alone in that tunnel during the final few minutes of regulation time. Ninety thousand screaming spectators, the television cameras—everything—slowly disappeared into the growing darkness around me. At the end of the regulation 90 minutes, going into the 2 minutes of added injury time, I expended every bit of my remaining concentration just to follow the flight of the Chinese corner kick sailing toward me in front of the net. I saw nothing but ball as I leaped to head it away. I didn't notice any of my opponents challenging me. I never saw or heard my own teammate, goalkeeper Brianna Scurry, charging off her line. When our paths intersected and Bri's arm smashed into the side of my head as she attempted to box the ball away, I had no idea who, or what, hit me.

Next thing I knew I was lying on the ground, my face pressed into the grass. I remember wanting to get up. But every time I tried to raise my head I started to pass out. I tried to move, but my entire body had quit working.

I felt no pain.

I'd survived harder blows to my head. That wasn't what kept me from getting back up. The problem was that I was now totally—physically, emotionally, and mentally—empty. Even the guts were gone.

Eventually someone lifted me up. While I was half-guided, half-carried from the field I thought I heard the word "overtime."

As badly as I'd wanted to finish this game, my teammates were now going to have to win or lose the world championship without me.

I spent the first bit of the initial 15-minute overtime period slumped on the U.S. bench, my eyes glazed. Doc Brown sat right beside me on the bench, helping hold me upright. Realizing I was more dangerously dehydrated than I'd first appeared, he summoned our team equipment manager, Dainis Kalnins, to help get me out of the heat.

It was only 4 or 5 minutes into overtime when I made the long, tedious trek from the bench to the tunnel at the end of the stadium. Dainis and another team physician, Dr. Mark Adams, each took an elbow and aimed me in the right general direction along the sideline. I was somehow able to keep my feet moving—but they were mostly carrying me.

I've seen the photos. I was not a pretty sight.

When they carried me into the medical treatment room under the stands, we were met by a team of EMTs (emergency medical technicians), nurses, and doctors who served as the Rose Bowl's medical staff. They laid me out on a table and Doc Adams quickly began his exam. By that time my blood pressure had plunged to the point that I could no longer control my thoughts or my feelings. I instinctively tried to curl into a ball as my oxygen-starved muscles contracted in violent cramps. My oxygen-deprived brain could no longer fight the pain or control my emotions.

I nearly blacked out. I felt a panicky, desperate need to fight for breath until someone slipped an oxygen mask over my face.

I wept in agony as someone cut off my game jersey and got it out of their way while Doc patiently tried to straighten my arm enough to insert the IV. One of the other medical folks in the room asked Doc if they should radio for a helicopter to medivac me to the nearest hospital ER.

⚽ ⚽ ⚽

"I don't think that will be necessary," Mark Adams informed his colleagues. He'd seen these symptoms before. "This is what happens with Michelle after a lot of games." He had already determined that she had not sustained a serious concussion from the blow to her head.

"I was concerned that the heat was making Michelle's usual exhaustion symptoms worse," the doctor recalls. "We

immediately turned a fan on her and cooled her with cold towels. That's why I cut her jersey off. And we started her usual postgame IV which would also provide an internal cooling off as we packed her extremities in iced towels."

The doctor soon began a second IV to try to stabilize her even more quickly. He knew the glucose-electrolyte solution would quickly ease the cramping and reduce Michelle's other symptoms. "Once we get a couple bags of fluid in her, she'll stabilize. We have to do this all the time with Michelle."

❀ ❀ ❀

With the IV finally in, as I relaxed enough to breathe normally and the fluids began slowly dripping into my arm, the tension in that treatment room also eased. The medical team turned some of their focus back onto the game playing on a small television set on a table across the room.

Slowly returning from wherever I'd been, I wanted to know what was happening. I wasn't yet mentally alert enough to follow the action on the screen. But I didn't need anyone to tell me the game was still going on. I knew by the constant roar of the crowd, rising and falling in a rumble I could feel as well as hear down in the depths of the stadium. I knew my teammates were still out there playing, and I desperately wanted to know how they were doing.

✵ ✵ ✵

Out on the field, Michelle's team wasn't doing so well without her. The Chinese dominated the overtime periods, but the Americans managed to hold China to a 0–0 tie and force the eventual penalty kick (PK) shoot-out. If Michelle had still been in the game at that point, Tony DiCicco would definitely have picked her to take one of the five PKs. Known for having the most powerful shot of any woman in the world, she'd long been the U.S. team's PK specialist. But this time, like millions of anxious Americans, Michelle could only wait and watch how the drama played out.

✵ ✵ ✵

Even then, as out of it as I was, I realized whatever happened, win or lose, this game wasn't going to be the end of my story. Any more than it was the beginning. . . .

Chapter Four
My Worst Loss

My parents could never tell me why. But the doctor who delivered me at a hospital in Santa Clara, California, on February 1, 1966, took one look at me and predicted, "You're gonna have your hands full with this girl; she's a stubborn one."

Before long, I lived up to the doctor's stubbornness prediction by showing remarkable determination in learning to walk. I refused to quit trying, no matter how hard, or how many times, I fell down. So by the time my brother Mike came along to complete our happy little family, I was already a hard-charging two-year-old terror with a lot of high speed miles behind me.

Looking back now I can see we must have been pretty poor at the time. Pops worked long hours as a meat-cutter at a local Safeway store while attending nearby San Jose State University. His goal was to someday become a professional counselor. Mom was a full-time home-maker who made most of our clothes on her sewing machine and served delicious made-from-scratch meals we ate together as a family at least twice a day.

We lived in a small subdivision where the cookie-cutter houses were packed so tightly together that when we looked out our kitchen window, we could see right through our neighbor's kitchen and into the next house two doors down. Our home sat on a corner lot, so we had a larger lawn than most of our neighbors. And Dad built a tree house out back that helped make our big yard the center of attraction for all the neighborhood kids.

So my earliest memories are warm ones—highlighted by plenty of family love and togetherness.

The four of us frequently attended Grandma and Grandpa's church with them. But more often we went by ourselves as a family. I hated wearing Sunday dresses even more than I dreaded having to sit still through the long, dry services. I believed in God, but it seemed the people I saw at church were about as cold, lifeless, and stiff as the old pews we sat in.

I never felt I could be myself in church, where it seemed everyone expected me to be a sweet little girl in a pretty dress, who read quietly, played with babies, and always stayed nice and neat. I definitely didn't fit that mold.

I liked our family times much better—whether I was helping Mom do gardening, holding nails for Dad when he tackled some carpentry project, or just watching over Dad's shoulder and handing him tools while he worked on his truck. I enjoyed spending time with my family. Especially after-dinner ball games with Pops and Mike out in the yard. We'd play whatever sport was in season.

When we were real young, football was our favorite. Dad would send Mike and me out for long "Hail Mary" passes until his arm got tired. I'd pretend to be Mean Joe Green snaring a touchdown pass from Terry Bradshaw. And I'd lie in bed at night dreaming about growing up someday to play for my favorite team—the Pittsburgh Steelers.

My favorite outfit—which I'd have worn to school every day if Mom had let me—was a pair of dark forest-green double-patch Tufskin jeans, Keds tennis shoes, and my official Steelers jersey with Mean Joe's number 75 clearly visible beneath the braids hanging down my back.

My love for sports wasn't always met with the same approval at school as it was in my family and among the neighborhood boys who regularly gathered in our yard to play.

I remember the day in third-grade PE when the boys stayed on the school playground for a kickball game while our teacher escorted all the girls to a nearby park to play on the swings. I told the teacher that (1) I wanted to play kickball, and (2) I wasn't going to the park to swing. Then I plopped myself down on the nearest park bench and refused to move.

The frustrated teacher sent me to the principal's office. My mother was called and asked to come to school for a conference and to take me home for the day. I sat outside by the secretary's desk while Mom and my principal held what seemed like a very long, closed-door meeting.

When Mom finally came out, she took me by the hand and we went home. But she and the principal evidently reached an understanding. The next day, and every day thereafter, my teacher allowed me to play kickball with the boys.

That was the same year Mom signed me up for my very first soccer team, the Cougars, and volunteered to be assistant coach herself. Since I was the only player unafraid of diving for the ball in the mud, the coach immediately made me goalkeeper.

I hated it.

Our team wore pink and yellow jerseys. Girlie colors. Yuck!

But what I despised even more than our uniforms was losing every game. Our team of eight-year-olds just couldn't compete with the nine- and ten-year-old teams in our league. Week after week we'd get slaughtered, and I'd cry all the way home, angrily declaring that I was *not* going to play the next week. But assistant coach Mom, and Dad, who came to cheer every game, refused to let me quit the team.

I suspect they hoped this soccer experience could help me channel my intensely competitive nature and learn to better control my anger at the same time. I definitely needed help in both areas.

Even by the age of eight, I was driven by the need to win. Whether it was the family playing Monopoly on the kitchen table or a tackle football game with neighborhood boys out in our yard, I *had* to come out on top. When I didn't, I would pout, stomp off, cry, slug the winner, or simply explode. I absolutely *hated* to lose—at anything.

I remember the day an older boy challenged me to a race at school. I knew I was the fastest kid in my grade. And I could outrun most of the boys in my neighborhood. But even though I suspected Greg could beat me, I wouldn't back down. The two of us lined up in actual racing lanes painted on the asphalt playground for what was probably a forty-yard sprint. A bunch of kids gathered to watch. Someone said, "On your mark, get set, GO!" And we took off.

Greg beat me across the finish line. But when he slowed down, I tackled him and beat him up. I got in trouble both at school and at home that day. And there were enough other temper-related playground incidents, involving everything from tetherball to four-square to jump rope, that my parents definitely knew I had trouble losing graciously.

However, my willingness to fight had its positive side as well. I remember standing in line waiting my turn during a kickball game one day at recess, when I saw my first-grade brother Michael running across the playground crying.

"M-m-michelle," he blubbered, pointing back the direction he'd come from. "That big kid over there said he was gonna beat me up. A-a-and he knows karate."

The kickball game had to wait while I marched across the school playground to confront the older boy who'd been bullying Mike. "Don't you pick on my brother!" I told him, punctuating my words with a shove.

I don't know if he'd seen me beat up Greg or he'd learned my reputation by talking to kids from the neighborhood. Or maybe he was just a cowardly bully. Whatever the reason, he immediately backed off. Message delivered, I trotted back to my kickball game before I lost my turn.

Our family moved to Seattle, Washington, the summer before fourth grade and shortly after Dad completed his college degree at San Jose State. He'd found a better job, as manager of the entire meat department for another Safeway. The new position enabled him to work days and attend graduate school classes at night at Seattle University. He also found us a bigger, two-story house in the old North Seattle neighborhood of Lake Forest Park. And that wasn't the only upside of the move for me.

Team sports proved a great way for me to meet and make new friends. And it seemed we moved into a real hotbed of youth soccer in the Northwest. So despite my less than positive first-year soccer experience back in Santa Clara, Mom signed me up for the Shorelake Soccer Club U–10 Thunderbirds.

The coach let me play center midfielder where I saw a lot more action than I'd ever had as goalkeeper and soon discovered I absolutely loved the game. It also helped that the Thunderbirds won far more games than we lost. And that the uniforms were a more acceptable color—green.

Mom got me to all my practices and volunteered as team mother. But Dad too came to every game, which I appreciated because his approval had always meant so much to me.

Pops had one habit that drove me nuts, though. On the rare occasions we did lose, I would get so angry I'd sit in the backseat and fume all the way home. Every time that happened my father would try to use his best (or worst) psychology to lighten my mood. Sometimes he'd try to tease me and make me laugh. That only made me angrier.

Then he'd resort to reasoning. "It's just a soccer game, Michelle."

Like I don't know that. That's not the point.

"Did you have fun, Michelle?"

"NO!" *Of course I didn't have fun. We lost! Losing is never fun!*

For such a smart guy I thought my Pops could be pretty dumb. *He just doesn't get it!*

As much as I hated to lose, I loved playing soccer even more. I loved to push myself. To go hard. To compete. To give everything I had. To overcome tough odds. And of course, to win.

Chapter Five

Sore Loser

laying with the Thunderbirds was fun. We spent most of every practice just scrimmaging, among ourselves or against an older Shorelake Soccer Club team. I thought that was a blast. I even enjoyed the running and the basic drills we did to improve our passing and dribbling skills. No matter how often or long the coach practiced us, I always wanted to do more.

Any day I couldn't persuade Michael and a few neighborhood friends to walk over to Brookside Elementary for a pickup game on the playground, I'd take a ball outside and practice on my own in the yard. I'd use the side of the house or the garage door for the goal and boom shots off it until my legs ached. Then I'd imagine our dog and my pet goat, Peter, as defenders while I dribbled over, under, around, and through the trees and bushes in our backyard. And after I wore out all opposing pets and vegetation, I'd juggle for awhile—always counting the number of times I could bounce the ball with my feet, my knees, and even off my chest and head without letting it hit the ground. I would forever compete—even if it was just against myself—trying to do everything harder, faster, or longer than I had the time before.

❂ ❂ ❂

In the summer of 1975, when she was nine years old, Michelle received a scholarship to spend a week at Northwest Soccer Camp out on Whidbey Island. "I remember vividly the first time I laid eyes on her," the camp director Cliff McCrath says. She looked like "a typical, spindly legged, somewhat impish nine-year-old. But that was where any comparison to a typical nine-year-old girl ended. Because she was playing soccer. And she took to the task with a vengeance . . . make that a fury. She not only despised losing, she hated anything that smacked of mediocrity. She wanted to be the best.

"To be perfectly honest she was a pest. She always wanted to do more. More shooting, more touches, more of whatever drills we were doing. She would wear the staff out.

"Her third year at our camp when Michelle was eleven, she took part in the finals of that week's juggling competition. We made the mistake of starting the contest late on the last morning. . . ."

This event usually took a very few minutes. And indeed on this day the balls began hitting the ground and everyone soon dropped out.

Everyone but Michelle ... who kept going strong. She'd bounce the ball off the top of one foot for a while, then switch to the other foot. Then she'd lift her knees and juggle the ball from one thigh to the other, occasionally lofting it high enough to bounce it off her head a time or two before catching it with her foot to start the routine all over again.

Other campers circled around to watch. Before long a few people tired of standing and took seats on the ground. Lunchtime came and hungry campers went, straggling off slowly in twos and threes. Somewhere along the line, Cliff McCrath had taken over counting for Michelle. "She'd long since shattered the camp record. But she wanted to go farther ... and farther. After an hour or so I think I was the only one remaining out there with her," he recalls. "Still she kept going."

All the way to 5,392 touches. "And she didn't miss the ball then," McCrath says. "Her neck got stiff, she got bored and hungry and simply decided to quit and go eat.

"That was Michelle. From the very beginning, she always defined for me what great athletes have that is not coachable. She had it inside her—total commitment, supreme effort, and disciplined determination."

But not all areas of her life were as positive for Michelle as sports were after the Akers family moved to Washington.

✵ ✵ ✵

I guess my parents had some rough times even when we lived in California. I was perhaps too young to notice back then. But tension in their marriage definitely increased after we moved to Seattle. Many were the nights I'd lie in bed up in my room and hear them arguing downstairs.

My mom applied to join the Kenmore Fire Department during my fifth-grade year. Other kids' mothers had unexciting jobs like teachers and secretaries. My mom was going to be a firefighter. I thought that was pretty cool. And when she became the first female firefighter in King County, Washington, I was extremely proud of her.

Yet the problems between my parents intensified. I'd pull the covers up over my head and try not to listen. But those arguments grew louder and more frequent. I didn't have to make out the words to know the anger behind them. The pain echoed through the entire house, up the stairs, and into my heart.

I remember one particular night in sixth grade when I decided I couldn't lie there and ignore it any longer. I climbed out of bed, slipped quietly downstairs, and hesitantly walked in on my parents in the den.

Everything got suddenly quiet. Mom said, "What are you doing up, Michelle? We thought you were asleep long ago."

"What's wrong?" Dad asked, noticing my tears. "Why are you crying?"

I told them I was afraid because, "I don't want you to get a divorce."

They both gave me big hugs and reassured me they weren't about to break up. I went back to bed feeling so relieved I fell right to sleep.

But on an even more memorable night, a short time later, Mike and I had already gone up to prepare for bed when our parents called us back downstairs. "We've got something we need to tell you," Mom said as they took us into the family room. I remember sitting on her lap in a big old rocking chair. She put her arms around me as she said, "Your dad and I have decided it will be best if we get a divorce."

My first reactions were shock and confusion. Then anger. *They lied to me.*

They assured us that it wasn't our fault. That they loved us both very much and always would. They told us they were still our mom and dad and we'd always be a family. But they explained Dad was going to be leaving that night. He was moving out. Though he assured us he would find a place to live nearby and see us as often as possible.

The more they tried to make it sound okay, the more upset I got. Michael and I were both crying when we went back upstairs and Pops began collecting a few of his personal belongings.

Minutes later I stood with my brother looking out of his upstairs bedroom window. Below in the darkness our father walked slowly to his truck in the rain with a single pillow tucked under his arm. We watched through our tears as he backed out of the driveway and drove off into the night.

Mike and I were still crying when Mom came upstairs to check on us a few minutes later. So she let us both sleep with her that night.

The next few nights my brother slept with me. And every evening for a long time after he'd begun sleeping in his room again, I'd lie in my bed and look out my door— across the hall into Mike's room. I'd see him kneeling there in front of his window. His hands folded in prayer, he'd be pleading with God to bring Dad home and put our family back together again. Night after night, I saw my little brother's pain as he bowed by that window, watching and waiting for God to answer his prayers.

I didn't bother to pray. I was angry at God. What did He care? Praying seemed to do no good.

Chapter Six
Walnut Wars

Even if I couldn't pray, I could at least hope that something would happen to bring my parents together again. Perhaps I could do more than just hope.

For months after our parents' separation, Mike and I carefully watched for the mailman every afternoon. Anytime we spotted a legal-sized envelope with Mom's attorney's return address, we swiped the envelope and threw it away long before Mom got home to check the mail.

Even then I think I knew we couldn't delay the process for long. Still, Mike and I grasped at any and every reason for hope.

I remember one time when our hopes were high. Our whole family was invited to some relative's wedding and all four of us sat together in one pew. Mom sat on one side of Mike and me, Dad sat on the other. At one point in the ceremony I recall noticing, out of the corner of my eye, that Mom and Dad had reached behind us and were actually holding hands. Mike and I exchanged looks and I thought, *They're gonna get back together for sure now.*

But after the wedding ended, nothing changed. We went home with Mom, and Pops headed for his apartment.

Mike and I both really missed our father. He lived close by so he could stay involved in our lives. He'd still come to all of our soccer games and school programs. We knew we could call if we needed him for anything—or just to talk. But it wasn't the same.

We looked forward to having our once-a-week supper with him, especially when he'd take us out to eat at Dairy Queen. We always ordered the biggest burgers, fries, Coke, and of course, a huge soft-serve ice cream concoction with enough extra hot fudge and peanuts that I crudely renamed it Peanut Butter Barf-ait because it contained enough sugar to make any kid sick.

Less exciting than DQ were Dad's home-cooked meals. For the longest time his kitchen skills limited him to hamburger—which he always overcooked into charred hunks of dry meat you had to drown in ketchup and gulp down with large swallows of water.

What his entree lacked, though, Dad made up for with dessert. While he cleaned up the kitchen after dinner he always sent us to the grocery store across the street from his apartment to buy a half-gallon of whatever kind of ice cream we wanted.

It would have been any kid's dream, except for one thing. Pops would always pull out an old coffee can full of change, count out the price of a half-gallon in pennies, nickels, and dimes. Embarrassed to walk into a store with a bagful of change, we'd always complain, "C'mon, Dad. Can't you give us some regular money?"

He'd always respond, "What are you talking about? Pennies are money, too."

Mike and I would finally give up and go to the store. And after arguing over what flavor (I always wanted mint chocolate chip), we'd look for the shortest checkout line and hand the cashier our bag of treasure. The clerks always said the same thing: "We can't take loose change like this. You need to get it rolled."

"We're sorry," we'd apologize. "This is all we have. Here, we'll help you count it." Meanwhile we were dying a thousand deaths as the line behind us quickly became the longest, and everyone in the store was looking at us like we had the plague or something. Once back home we'd recount our adventure to Dad, insisting that he get his pennies rolled so we wouldn't look so stupid next time.

Pops would just chuckle. "You got the ice cream, didn't you?"

Every other weekend we'd spend with Dad doing something fun—going to soccer games, hiking, camping, taking a ferry over to Bainbridge Island. He really worked to maintain his relationship with us.

The year after he and Mom broke up, he finally completed work on his master's degree. Mike and I got to see him graduate. I took pictures to record the occasion. Then we took him out to celebrate at a fancy-schmantzy restaurant on the waterfront in downtown Seattle.

We knew this was a big deal. Dad had only been able to go to school part-time because he'd had to work and support us, too. So it had been a long haul. We were very proud that he'd reached his goal.

Yet no matter how much fun and laughter we shared with him, despite his personal and professional accomplishments and how hard he tried to act as if nothing had changed, Dad could never quite completely disguise his deep, underlying sadness. I couldn't help feeling sorry for him.

Mom didn't seem to have the same trouble adjusting to the end of their marriage. Perhaps because her whole life was changing at once.

Where Dad made a gradual career change over the next couple of years, continuing to work for Safeway as a meat department manager while beginning to develop a part-time counseling practice, Mom made a much more sudden transformation. From homemaker to firefighter.

I was proud of her too. The fact that she accomplished something most women wouldn't think of attempting made me believe anything was possible. As the first woman in her department, Mom took a lot of grief. But she refused to back down. She was passionate and committed—two traits I inherited from her.

Of course I inherited just as much of my makeup from my Pops. The same kind of dogged persistence that kept him pursuing his dream of a career in psychology from the time I was born until I was thirteen years old has served me well over the course of a long soccer career. So, in truth, I inherited a good measure of strength and stubbornness from both parents.

Unfortunately, at the very time I began sorting out who I was and understanding how I was like and different from my parents, they were both gone. At least they didn't play the same role in my day-to-day life they always had.

As a firefighter, Mom worked a crazy schedule. She'd be on duty for twenty-four straight hours, then off for forty-eight. She'd leave for the station in the morning before we went to school and we wouldn't see her again until we got home from school the next afternoon. Mom always called in the afternoons to make sure we got home from school okay. And she usually had a casserole or something else she'd fixed and left in the fridge for us to heat up for supper. She did a good job of making us feel cared for and accountable.

As a by-product of our unusual new family schedule, I gained a larger measure of independence and responsibility than most twelve-year-olds. And it happened not gradually—but overnight.

We'd always been required to do chores. But when Mom went to work we were forced to step up our responsibility. I took charge of the household when she wasn't there. Mike and I both set our own alarms to get ourselves up and off to school. We'd fix breakfast and pack our own lunches every morning. In the afternoons we usually had a list of chores Mom had left for us— vacuuming, dusting, washing dishes, doing laundry.

It wasn't all work. Neither was it all positive. We had to learn to settle our own disputes and cope with our own cuts and bruises. And there were plenty of those, since Mike and I were still kids.

One time when we were grounded and not allowed to go outside, we figured Mom would never know. We sneaked out to play on a rope swing our neighbors had attached high in an evergreen tree. Being the daredevil I always was, I sprinted as hard as I could and swung higher and farther out than ever before. When I came down I crashed into a stump that caught me square on the shin. I fell to the ground screaming, rolling around in pain.

Mike, not knowing what else to do, figured he'd ease my pain by swinging on the rope and making faces to get me to laugh. I was in so much agony I couldn't even sit up, and here was my brother swinging back and forth above me acting like a monkey.

It worked. I told him to keep it up for a while. Then he dragged me back to the house and we waited for Mom to come home. She took one look at my shin, which by that time had swollen to the size of a black and blue grapefruit, and rushed me in for x-rays. The doctor told us no bone was broken, but he'd never seen an injury that serious without a break. It seemed to take forever to heal.

We instigated our share of other minor mischief. And it seemed we always got caught. Like the time our Aunt Gini down in California sent walnuts to our family for Christmas. We had piles of them. So while Mom was at work one day, Mike and I staged a walnut war in the living room with some neighborhood kids. We rearranged the couch and other furniture as bunkers behind which we stored our ammo in piles and threw the nuts at each other with all our might. Walnuts exploded against walls, shells flew everywhere. Occasionally we even hit each other. When we ran out of walnuts, the war was over.

We were smart enough to realize we needed to clean up after our escapade. So we put all the furniture back in place and started vacuuming up the shell fragments. We noticed the burning smell just before the vacuum quit. Apparently there were more than just fragments.

No matter what we did, we couldn't dislodge the walnut stuck in the vacuum. So we carefully crawled around on the floor picking up all the bits of walnut shell we could find with our fingers and then stored the machine away in the closet. As if Mom would never vacuum again.

A few days later Mom pulled out the sweeper and when it didn't work, she took it apart to find the jammed shell and half a vacuum bag full of broken walnuts. She naturally asked us what had happened. And I was such a bad liar that she had the truth out of me in no time and put me on restriction again, sending me to my room. She says she found walnuts in the furniture, the curtains, and scattered in odd places around the house for months afterwards.

Chapter Seven
And Bigger Trouble

On the surface at least, Mom appeared to have put her divorce behind her quicker and more easily than anyone else in our family. A year or so after the divorce, she married a man she'd met through work. And the going got pretty tough for a while.

Mike didn't like the guy from the start. I figured my brother just resented the idea that anyone else could replace Dad. I thought Mom deserved an opportunity to be happy just as much as anyone else. But I too soon decided happiness wasn't going to be part of this marriage either. And that was the way it turned out for the next couple years, before Mom divorced again.

During this time, one of the ways I escaped the tension and the turmoil of my own life was through reading. I'd shut my bedroom door, lie on my bed eating chocolate I should have been selling as a soccer team fund raiser, and lose myself in the fictional world of the Black Stallion series. I loved the adventures of Alec and the black. I used to dream it was me riding the Black Stallion and he was my horse. *Someday,* I told myself, *I want to have my own horse ranch.*

Another godsend during this time of my life was my friendship with Amy Major. We'd met when I first moved to Seattle back in fourth grade. The two of us tore it up on the soccer field where Amy played left wing and I was a center midfielder. We went to school together and lived in the same neighborhood. I spent so much time with Amy that her house and family became my second home. I ate over there, slept there, hung out there, and grew up there. Her parents and five sisters made it a place where I could get lost, have fun, be taken care of, and not have to worry about the chaos or pain of my own home life.

During those years my most consistent coping strategy for forgetting my troubles and ignoring the emotions eating my insides was to stay active. Whether that meant doing something with friends or just playing in the yard with my dog, I tried to keep moving. And sports were by far the best way I knew to do that.

I spent hours every day either on the soccer field, a baseball diamond, a basketball court, in our backyard, or just out on the street—playing whatever sport or activity happened to be going on.

Mom used to have to call me in for dinner and again at dark. Even then I responded only grudgingly. Better than any other therapy, sports were where I could lose myself and forget about the tough stuff going on in my life, expend pent-up emotions, stretch myself physically and mentally, have fun, and compete.

When we chose sides for neighborhood games, I was usually the first one picked. Often I'd be the only girl playing—which was fine with me; I could play harder against boys. And that made me that much tougher.

The soccer field in particular became an island of normality in the stormy sea of my life. Being a soccer star provided acceptance and affirmation. And no matter how disrupted and unsettled the rest of my life felt, the soccer field was one place I could be in control.

⚽ ⚽ ⚽

After moving to Washington, Michelle played four years with the Shorelake Thunderbirds, a club team which won several state and regional championships. By age fourteen she had already made such a name for herself in Seattle soccer circles that Michelle was invited to join the Union Bay Flyers, one of the strongest under-nineteen teams in the Pacific Northwest.

That meant she'd be playing with and competing against older girls who were much bigger and stronger than she was. Michelle gladly accepted that challenge; she knew from experience that tough competition would only make her better.

☻ ☻ ☻

As for my peers at school and in the neighborhood, the guys treated me like I was just one of the gang. If I teamed up with boys who didn't know me, I might have to tackle some dude, steal the ball, or score a couple quick goals to show them I could play. It usually wasn't long before I earned their respect and acceptance. If they started playing really rough because they were embarrassed a girl could beat them, I usually knew that the coach or some of the players or my brother would be there to make sure things didn't get out of hand. So it seldom took very long before I could just play and forget all about the guy-girl thing.

Playing with and against older girls on the U–19 Flyers very quickly elevated my game. And I remember the satisfaction I felt the very first time we scrimmaged a local women's team called the FC Lowenbraus, who won national adult amateur championships several years in a row. After stripping the ball from one of their players, I dribbled down the sideline toward their goal. As I ran past their coach on the sidelines, I could hear him screaming at his team, "Don't let that little girl beat you!"

I guess I *was* still a "little girl." At fourteen I was only average size for my age—maybe a little small. And playing on a team made up mostly of eighteen- and nineteen-year-olds, several of whom were six feet tall, suddenly made me feel my immaturity in other areas as well.

Going to parties with my teammates exposed me to beer for the first time. I thought it was fun to try something new and adult and crazy. Since my teammates only invited me to a few parties and my mom seldom let me go when they did, I had to devise my own strategy for acquiring booze.

I remember the first time a friend and I sneaked into my dad's house when I knew he would be gone. The two of us consumed most of a bottle of bourbon and got falling-down drunk. I threw up, scraped my knees badly, and ended up feeling pretty stupid. Several hours must have passed before we sobered up enough to call my friend's parents to ask for a ride home. At least I assume we'd sobered up. Her folks never said a word or even hinted that they knew what had been going on.

Emboldened by that experience, my friends and I would frequently swipe beer out of our families' refrigerators. Or we'd empty vodka bottles before carefully refilling them to the same level with water.

Some of my friends got another kind of kick from petty shoplifting; so I went along a few times. I never got caught doing that or another little trick we had of skipping out of restaurants without paying for our meals. But after messing around like that for while, my sense of integrity and personal honor crept in. I'd only wanted to be accepted and liked, but I began to feel ashamed of myself. I realized, *That's not who I am, or who I want to be.* Once I decided that kind of behavior was stupid and could only get me in trouble, I stopped hanging around those friends.

My parents didn't know about any of this, so they never seemed particularly worried about me and this kind of delinquent adolescent behavior. They did, however, know and express concern about my blossoming social life and the sudden attraction I had for a certain nineteen-year-old boy. The five-year age difference troubled my folks. And the red flags really went up when my usual good grades suddenly dropped.

Mom and Dad actually united in their insistence that I was seeing far too much of my new boyfriend. They sometimes refused to let me go out with him and even restricted me from soccer practice because they knew he and I could get together there.

I got into some loud screaming matches with my mom over this. I wanted to do what I wanted to do, and I decided anyone who got in my way would have to pay for it.

Mom's second marriage was clearly coming to an end during this period. At the same time, Dad finally seemed to be making progress in his life. He had expanded his cooking skills beyond blackened burgers to include beef stroganoff and meat loaf. That definitely improved the menu options each week when we had dinner at his house. He had a full-time counseling position and seemed well on his way to becoming a whole new man.

But when he teamed up with Mom to express concern over the relationship with my boyfriend, I didn't think either one of them had any right to interfere in my life. I felt like they were trying to control me. So I determined to ignore their concerns.

Dad refused to let my obstinate bitterness push him away. He kept coming to my games, fixing me dinner once a week, and having Mike and me over to his house every other weekend. Any day we didn't see him, he'd call to talk. If there had just been another blowup with Mom over my boyfriend, I wouldn't want to speak to him and was often angry enough that I didn't. He'd ask a question and I'd just hold the receiver to my ear in silence. Dad would say his piece and then he'd tell me, "I love you, Michelle."

When I didn't respond to that, he'd tell me, "I'm not hanging up until you say 'I love you' back to me."

Sometimes I was too stubborn to give in and I'd hang up on him. He'd always call back and I'd know I was in big trouble.

Part of me would feel guilty about treating my father that way. But I was too angry about everything that had happened in our family to apologize or admit that I really loved my dad and didn't want to be mad or mean to him. However, when I would finally give in and say "I love you," I didn't often sound like I meant it.

My confrontations with Dad upset my brother. Mike got mad at me because he saw how much my behavior was hurting our dad. Sometimes he'd take out that anger on me by sneaking into my room and turning all my pictures around just to annoy me. One day Mike found an even more original and memorable way to express his displeasure.

That evening I found a horde of huge, dead grasshoppers strewn all around my bedroom. On my bed, under my covers, among my folded clothes in drawers, even smashed in my schoolbooks. For a while there I wanted to squash my brother. And for a lot longer than that, I wondered if I'd have a decent relationship with anyone in my family ever again.

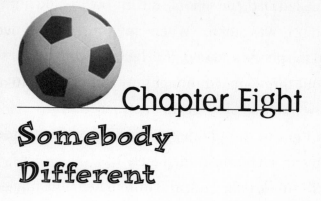

Chapter Eight

Somebody Different

My new boyfriend played such a big role in my life because I desperately wanted to feel like someone loved and accepted me just the way I was. And he did more than that, telling me how wonderful I was, agreeing that my parents were being unreasonable and that I had a right to run my own life. The fact that he was nineteen and good-looking didn't hurt either.

I'd never had a real boyfriend before. This love stuff all seemed new and exciting and mysterious to me. I'd started cutting school and sneaking over to his house to spend the day alone with him.

I doubt anyone suspected what was going on—until Mom found a note I'd accidentally dropped in the driveway. The handwritten excuse explained that "Michelle has been home sick with the flu this week." At the bottom I'd forged my mother's signature.

Mom called Dad, the school, and my boyfriend's home suspecting I was there. When my boyfriend's dad answered the phone and said, "Michelle, it's your mother," I just about threw up. I'd thought my scheme was fool-proof; now it was all blowing up in my face.

When I got to the phone, Mom didn't waste words. "Hang up and get home immediately!"

I did. Terrified, ticked off, and humiliated, I hightailed it home to face the music. And then I had to go and face the school authorities.

I had plenty of free time those next few weeks to think about what a mess my entire life had become. It seemed I was in trouble all the time and never knew how or when I'd get caught next. My brother hated me and resented Mom for divorcing our father. My mom was mad and no longer trusted me. And I wasn't even having much fun with my dad anymore. Tension had gotten so bad at home I hated to walk in the front door. My first quarter report card stunk. I'd gotten in trouble with my principal, and my parents had totally restricted me from my boyfriend and from soccer practice with the Flyers. *Everything I try to do turns out wrong.*

The only adult I felt I could talk to at that time was my English teacher, Al Kovats. He was the "coolest" teacher at Shorecrest; and I wasn't the only one who thought so.

Mr. Kovats coached boy's soccer at Shorecrest. He came to watch all my soccer games the fall of my freshman year.

And he'd talk to me about the game when I came to class the next day. He was so nice and such a relief from all the other adults in my life that I just liked hanging out in his classroom during his planning period. We'd read soccer books together and he'd draw plays on the board.

What intrigued me most about this man wasn't his love of soccer. There was something else about him that made him stand out. He was outgoing and friendly, but it was more than that. He had an air of self-confidence and inner joy that I envied. I felt like such a failure in my personal life that I had a hard time imagining I could ever be happy again. So how did Mr. Kovats do it? What made the guy tick?

After I started to get to know him, I came right out and asked him. "What's your deal, Mr. Kovats? Why are you always so upbeat?"

He told me it was because he was a Christian.

He wasn't like any Christian I'd encountered before. He actually seemed to be excited about his faith.

I told him I hadn't been to church much since we'd moved to Seattle. That I believed God was probably out there, but all the times I'd ever asked Him for help, He'd never shown up. So He obviously couldn't have cared less about me. On top of that, the only thing anyone seemed to get out of religion and church anyway was a chance to go to heaven after you die. And that just wasn't doing it for me at that point in my life.

So why in the world was Kovats excited about God? I didn't get it.

But there must be something there.

Mr. Kovats told me Christianity wasn't so much a religion as it was a relationship—a personal relationship with God through Jesus Christ. That God was a friend who loved him. And vice versa. That's what he was excited about, that's where his confidence came from: just knowing that he had a personal relationship with the Creator of the universe was the entire basis of his attitude toward life.

He made it sound so real I could almost believe it. I knew he believed it. And I wanted to trust him.

I began to tell him about my parents' divorce and the strained relationships with everyone in my family. We talked about school. I even told him about my boyfriend. So Mr. Kovats knew my life was a mess and he heard my discouragement about it.

He was as honest with me as I was with him. He told me flat out he thought my boyfriend was taking me for a ride. He also told me that if I would accept Jesus Christ into my heart and life and let Him take control of my life, that God would help me change a lot of those things that were bothering me and also help me deal with any problems I couldn't change.

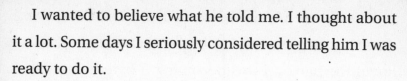

I wanted to believe what he told me. I thought about it a lot. Some days I seriously considered telling him I was ready to do it.

Two factors kept me from it.

I worried about what other people would think. Will my friends still accept me if I say I'm a Christian? I sure didn't want to be a nerd or a religious freak.

The other barrier I faced was actually fear. I was just plain scared to make that kind of commitment. My parents' divorce had rocked my confidence; I found it difficult to really trust anyone or anything. To hope what Mr. Kovats said about God being able to help me change the mess I was in seemed too big a risk to take. If I committed to this and it didn't work out, if it turned out even God couldn't help me, then where would I be? There might be no hope left at all. What then?

One day during basketball season, Mr. Kovats, who was assistant girls' coach, offered to drive me home. Since my alternative was walking three miles home in the dark (which I did on occasion when Mom was working), I gladly accepted. He often gave several kids a lift. But on this particular day it was just the two of us when he pulled his beat-up, rusted-out, lime-green pickup truck to a stop in my driveway.

We sat there talking like we often did. This time I broke down and began to cry my heart out. I told Mr. Kovats I hated the person I was becoming. I hated what I was doing to my family. I hated everything going on inside of me. I was angry. I was confused.

He listened quietly and then he said, "Michelle, I've told you everything I have to tell you. I don't know anything else to say."

"I need a relationship with God like you have. How do I get that?"

He smiled and told me all I needed to do was ask. It was that simple. And there in the front seat of his old pickup, with rain splattering on the windshield, he took my hand, we bowed our heads, and I repeated a prayer that went something very much like this:

"Dear Jesus, I know I've messed up. I need Your help. I can't do it on my own. I want to know You. And I want to welcome You into my life. Amen."

I don't know how to explain what happened, but as I prayed it was like a swoosh of warmth went all through me. I thought, *Wow! Something is really happening.* I didn't know what. I just took a deep breath and all that stuff that was going on inside me before was gone.

I got a feeling much like I'd experienced many times at the end of a daylong hike through the mountains with my dad and Michael, when I'd finally drop the sixty-pound pack I'd been carrying for miles. Suddenly I realized the exhausting weight I'd grown so accustomed to wasn't really a part of me after all. I'd slipped it off. It was gone. And I felt so free and strong and good.

Mr. Kovats grinned and told me this could be a fresh start for me.

I climbed out of his truck and headed inside to face my angry family and the mess I'd made. I still wasn't sure what had just happened. But even walking in the front door, I knew something was different. I didn't feel like the same sad, lost, angry person I'd been before. The frustration and fear had gone.

It wasn't something other people could see. They might not even realize it right away, but from that moment on, I knew I was a different person inside. That evening marked a turning point in who I was and how I determined to live my life.

Chapter Nine

Playin' with the Big Boys

I certainly didn't become a sudden saint. But a lot of things did begin to change. I no longer skipped school, and I soon quit drinking and partying. My grades came back up. I even broke off the relationship with my boyfriend. My brother and I got along much better.

Of course I still had some of the normal disagreements most teenagers have with parents as they work out their own family's definition of independence and maturity. I was still pretty stubborn. But I didn't have the constant, bitter conflicts with my folks that I'd had the past few years. I started spending time with my dad because I wanted to, not because I had to. And I found it easier to tell him I loved him. Sometimes without any prompting.

I started attending church with Mr. Kovats and his family who belonged to a nondenominational congregation. Much to my surprise, I liked it, learned a lot, and actually looked forward to going. Unlike my experience as a child, this church seemed neither stiff nor boring.

Still trying to figure out what all it meant to be a Christian and have a personal relationship with God, I got very excited and learned a lot when I joined a young peoples' Bible study discipleship class. I even began to understand the Bible a little bit more as I met and talked with other people who said they wanted to follow Jesus.

My decision to ask Christ into my life changed my heart. The anger and discouragement I'd felt for so long were gone.

As other areas of my life became less troublesome, I found I had even more energy to channel into sports.

⚽ ⚽ ⚽

Michelle had tried out for the varsity soccer team her freshman year, scared to death she wouldn't make it. But she did. The coach didn't actually start her the first game of the season—something about not wanting a ninth-grader to get too cocky. From then on, no coach in his right mind could have kept her on the bench. She started as center midfielder every game the next four years for the Shorecrest High School Scots. Michelle's team won several metro championships and her senior year they took the state championship despite the fact that a severely sprained ankle forced Michelle to play the entire final game one-

*legged. She made High School All-American her sopho-
more, junior, and senior years.*

*In the state of Washington, high school girls' teams
played soccer in the fall. The boys played a spring season. So
the spring of Michelle's sophomore year, Al Kovats invited
her to work out and practice with his boys' team. He says,
"I thought the physical competition she would get playing
regularly with high school boys would strengthen her and
teach her to deal with the more physical style of play I knew
she would eventually encounter on the college level."*

✿ ✿ ✿

He was right. I learned a lot about playing and surviving hard-nosed soccer. Mr. Kovats also worked with me
one-on-one to improve and perfect my heading tech-
nique. And he taught me the basic mentality and strategy for penalty kicks I still use. He taught me to be
consistent in my placement. Before I kick, he told me, I
needed to pick a side and never change my mind in mid-
approach. He also taught me to practice my PKs. A lot.

In addition to the soccer experience I got at school, I
continued to play with my club team, the U–19 Flyers,
most of the rest of the year. It was there that I honed my
skills and began to gain notice on a national level.

So soccer played a huge role in my life during those
teenage years. I invested countless hours and measureless

energy in the sport. But it gave me so much more in return.

It was on the soccer field, more than in any other part of my life, that I got hooked into lasting friendships. At the same time I felt special and apart from the crowd.

Soccer left me with a wealth of rich memories. Sure I went to the prom; the fact that I actually wore a dress helped make that a newsworthy event. And I can still picture the school halls and a few teachers' faces in my mind's eye. But the most vivid and memorable moments from my high school years involve soccer.

Soccer even provided me a stepmother. Sue Separovich officiated some of the games my club teams played. The first time I ever said anything to her she gave me a yellow card for mouthing off during a game. I got to know Sue better during high school when her daughter Shelley, who was a couple grades behind me, played with me on the Shorecrest varsity.

She seemed like such a cool, with-it lady that one time in a bus on our way to an out-of-town tournament I was talking to Sue when a thought hit me: "You know," I said, "I'd really like to see you and my dad get together."

Sue looked at me like I was crazy, because she and Dad were just casual friends. So I told her, "I mean it. I think you guys would be great together."

Sue thanked me. "I think it's really nice you feel that way, Michelle. But I don't think it's ever going to happen." She was wrong.

Of course it took a little more encouragement—and another two years. They eventually began dating my senior year in high school and got married the following fall.

In a way I can say soccer gave me a whole new family. Complete with a new sister and brother (John was a year older than I), as well as a stepmother who became a very important person in my life and in my father's.

Soccer also offered me recognition and acclaim. But seeing my name and picture in the papers seemed to mean more to family and friends than it did to me. The trophies and the attention were nice, but I didn't play for awards or public praise. I played because I loved the game. I loved to compete.

I just wanted to play soccer whenever and wherever I could. I actually missed my own high school graduation to play in a tournament with the Flyers. I never thought twice about the decision.

I was already looking to the future. I wasn't a high school student any longer. I was still, and first of all, a soccer player.

Soccer gave me an identity.

# Chapter Ten

Full Speed Ahead

One other thing soccer provided for me: a college education.

From the end of my junior year through the fall of my senior year of high school, I was contacted by schools all over the country. After struggling with the decision for months, I finally accepted a scholarship from the University of Central Florida in Orlando.

While I felt good about my choice, I wrestled with mixed emotions in August of 1984 when it came time to get on the airplane that would take me three thousand miles away from home to school. I cried saying good-bye to my family. I thought, *What am I doing? I don't know a soul in Florida! What if no one likes me? What if I stink as a soccer player? What makes me think I'm even smart enough for college? Do I really have what it takes?*

Walking through the door of the jetway I felt as if I was journeying into the great unknown—all alone. Yet an exciting sense of adventure and challenge enabled me to overcome my fears and board my flight.

✪ ✪ ✪

On the very first day of practice, Coach Jim Rudy put his fastest veteran defender on Michelle. When Michelle beat her, he switched to his toughest, hardest-hitting defensive player who could kick an opponent into the stands. Michelle took her lumps, got up, and beat that player as well. Years later Jim Rudy would say that by the time he realized no one on his nationally ranked team could even slow Michelle down, let alone prevent her from scoring, he knew she was going to be something special.

✪ ✪ ✪

From the beginning, I was very impressed by the intensity of the college game. But I didn't know quite what to think that first season when we played our biggest rival, number-one-ranked North Carolina. Apparently the UNC players had heard something about me, because, from the opening kickoff, they slammed and grabbed me whenever I got near the ball. One of the first times I went up for a headball, a Tar Heel knocked me clear over the touchline. As I picked myself up off the Carolina-blue track and started back onto the field she snarled, "Welcome to college soccer!" A little later in the game another opponent seized me from behind and hurled me to the ground—breaking my bra in the process.

Though surprised by the physical competitiveness of college soccer, I was more fired up than intimidated. *If that's the way the game is played—great!* I knew I had the fire in me, too.

Just like in high school, I couldn't seem to get enough soccer. I'd go out early every afternoon from one to two o'clock for goalkeeper practice. That gave me extra time to work on my shooting. We'd have our regular team practice from two to four. Then, since Jim Rudy also coached the UCF men's soccer team, he sometimes let me stay and work out with the guys from four to six.

But the demands of soccer didn't leave a lot of time during the season for much of a social life, and the upperclassmen on our team didn't have anything to do with us off the field anyway. So my roommate Amy All-mann (who was also from Seattle) and I were left to entertain ourselves.

I'd asked my dad to ship my bicycle from Seattle. It arrived safe and sound in a huge bike box big enough for two people to fit in. So Amy and I got this brilliant idea.

We pulled the box over our heads and cut small holes near the top so we could see out. Then we'd take the box out on campus at night and hide in it. We called it SWAT-ing—for Seattle Washington Attack Team. While no one was around we'd get in the box, lean it against some wall, and wait for people to come by. Once they weren't looking we'd stand up, move the box, and set it back down again. When they'd suddenly see it in a different place they'd think they were losing their minds.

Or we'd lean it up next to a pay phone and try not to crack up listening to some guy whispering lovey-dovey stuff to his girlfriend. That was a riot. When we weren't out SWATing, we hid the box behind this giant wall hanging in our room. And we didn't tell anyone else about it.

One night we were out SWATing very late when we spotted one of our teammates coming out of the library. So we started stalking her. When she'd look back we'd stop. She'd start walking and we'd pick up the box and move again. Every time she looked over her shoulder we'd freeze. She walked faster and faster. Then we started chasing her. She took off running across campus, screaming bloody murder with us in the box running after her, laughing so hard we could hardly stay on our feet.

She didn't tell anyone what had happened until one afternoon at practice a couple weeks later. "You guys are going to think this is weird," she told the whole team.

"But one night when I was coming home from the library, this box started chasing me." Sure enough, a bunch of players laughed at her. Amy and I never said a word.

Nobody suspected a thing until I gave a talk in speech class on the topic "How to SWAT in a Bike Box." I received an F for my effort, in part because I wasn't a very good public speaker, but mostly because the teacher thought I was making the whole thing up. The assignment had called for a true how-to speech and he insisted there was no way two people could fit in a bike box.

I brought Amy and the box to class to prove him wrong. The prof changed my grade, but we'd blown our cover. So we had to find other ways to get our kicks off the field.

In the spring of my freshman year, I received a letter from the U.S. Soccer Federation, officially inviting me to a tryout for a U.S. national women's soccer team that would be going to Europe for an international tournament later that summer.

Looking back I realize I should have felt honored. That 1985 U.S. Women's National Team was a true first for American soccer. Never before had any women's soccer team officially represented our country in international competition. But it didn't seem like a particularly big deal to me. As far as I was concerned, this was just another chance to play soccer. That's why I decided to go.

To be honest, the whole experience had the feel of an amateur all-star squad. We didn't even get together until early August for a four-day camp in upstate New York before we boarded a plane and flew to Italy for the tournament. We even looked like an amateur all-star team, wearing old hand-me-down men's uniforms.

The other countries' teams were so much more fit and soccer savvy that we seemed to play like amateurs in comparison—chasing them futilely all over the field. Plus most of our opponents already had valuable international experience, playing a much more physical style than any of us Americans had ever experienced. The first time a defender flew into my knees with her cleats up, making no attempt to go for the ball, I realized I was in a battle. The other teams grabbed our shorts and yanked our hair on breakaways. They punched and stomped and kicked and actually spit in our faces. And inexperienced amateurs that we were, we angrily complained in vain to the referee, foolishly thinking we could expect a fair call from a ref when we were playing a team from his country. We eventually got mad and retaliated, only to earn ourselves a few yellow and red cards.

But despite our opponents' superior skill and our own glaring lack of international experience, our American team scrapped and fought and kept the scores respectable. Italy beat us in our very first game by a score of 1–0. Three days later we tied Denmark 2–2—the game in which I scored the first-ever U.S. Women's National Team goal.

Two days later, after traveling from Jesolo to Caorle, Italy, we lost a 3–1 match to England in which I scored the only U.S. goal and suffered a dislocated shoulder when I got taken down hard on a late-game tackle. I wanted to play despite the pain, but after the extent of my injury was known, I sat out our last game of that tournament—a 0–1 loss to Denmark.

We all went home realizing we had a lot of work to do if we wanted to compete against the best of the world. But no one ever said anything about getting together again. So I didn't know that we ever would.

I arrived back in Florida just a couple days before preseason training began that fall of my sophomore year. But I injured my knee and ended up sitting out the entire season.

Chapter Eleven
New School Ties

The highlight of my college soccer career came my junior year when we went on a twelve-game winning streak that carried through the end of the regular season and into the playoffs. We breezed through the opening rounds to win our regional and reach the Final Four. I played well enough to be named offensive MVP of the tournament. But what I'll always remember best about the entire experience will be playing the NCAA semifinals in the worst soccer conditions I have ever experienced.

We'd arrived in Massachusetts to practice on a nice fall day. A cold front blew through that night and temperatures plunged to all-time lows. We wore nylons, sweatpants, and three layers of shirts under our uniforms. We played in mittens and hats—and one of our players still got a frostbitten ear. They set up gas-jet blowers for heat along the sidelines by the benches. Another of our players actually melted a shoe trying to thaw her feet at halftime. There was just no way to keep warm when the game-time windchill measured something like thirty degrees below zero.

Our personal physical discomfort was only part of the problem. The surface of the field froze so solid it felt like we were playing on a concrete parking lot. I slide-tackled a girl in a patch of frozen mud that ripped a huge gash on my knee. Looking down at the blood soaking through the tear in my pants I remember thinking, *That should hurt!* But my legs were so numb with cold I didn't feel a thing.

The ball felt like a ten-pound shot from a cannon when it hit you. And moving it around the field was like kicking a cement block. The cold and wind got so bad that several of Amy Allmann's goalkeeper punts never crossed the eighteen-yard line. Needless to say, neither team managed to mount much of an attack.

The score was tied 1–1 when UMass finally managed a shot on goal with only a few minutes remaining, Amy couldn't react fast enough to do a thing. When we ended up losing the game by the score of 2–1, the disappointment over the loss was greatly overshadowed by the frustration of having had to play under such terrible conditions.

❀ ❀ ❀

The Golden Knights didn't go quite as far in 1988 when Michelle was a fifth-year senior. UCF ended a 10–3–2 season with a tough 2–1 loss in the NCAA region final to North Carolina. But she had what may have been her best season as a collegian. She led her team in scoring again, setting an all-time school career scoring record. She won All-American honors for the fourth time in her college career and received the 1988 Hermann Trophy as the national college player of the year.

❀ ❀ ❀

But the absolute best part of my entire college experience was the friendships I made with people like Lisa Gozley and Laurie Hayden. Goz, Hades, and Akes. The three of us became so inseparable we dressed up for Halloween one year as Snap, Crackle, and Pop—the Rice Krispie elves.

We always had a special chemistry between us—a major element of which was laughter. And some of our best laughs came at each others' expense. Goz and Hades used to gang up on me sometimes. They'd make fun of me for every reason you could think of. For example, we planned to bake a cake for some party, so we went to the grocery to get everything we needed. When I started collecting flour, eggs, cocoa, oil, and so forth, they said, "WHAT are you doing, Akes?"

"Buying stuff to make the cake," I replied.

They practically laughed their heads off before they insisted, "Let's just buy a mix."

"Okay," I agreed reluctantly. Mom always cooked from scratch and I'd learned to bake from her. But when I started gathering ingredients for frosting (powdered sugar, shortening, etc.) they burst out laughing again.

"Let's just get canned frosting," they insisted.

"What?" I didn't even know you could buy frosting in a can. Goz and Hades thought that was the funniest thing yet and called me Betty Crocker for a long time after that.

They also nicknamed me "Grace" because I was always stumbling over stuff and banging into things. They made fun of me forever after I crashed my bike into a garbage dumpster. "How did you not see that huge green metal box right in front of you?" Goz demanded to know. She and Hades thought it absolutely hilarious that an All-American soccer player could be such an accident-prone klutz off the field. But I was. I figured it was genetic, since my dad is the same way. So I had to laugh with them.

They also teased me mercilessly for always being slow to get things—whether it was a new drill or an old joke.

The coach would explain some play and then ask me if I understood it. "Huh? What?" was such a frequent response that it became a team punch line. Even the coach would mimic my "Huh? What?"

Sometimes when they thought I was acting more dense than usual, Hades or Goz would say, "Hey, Akes! Do we need to pump a little more air in your head?" And we'd all laugh.

Yet underneath the laughter, the constant ribbing, and the good-natured put-downs there was a deep, mostly unspoken commitment to one another. Goz used to help me study for classes. She was an instant memorizer. But where I could learn the gist of material quickly enough, I had real trouble remembering specifics like words and definitions. So Goz would spend hours working to help me memorize body parts for an anatomy test when I was struggling big time with that class. When I ended up with a B, she was as thrilled as I was.

Of all the significant things my years at UCF afforded me—a good college education, numerous athletic awards, many wonderful memories on and off the field—what I will always treasure most from that exciting time in life is the friendships I shared with some very special teammates.

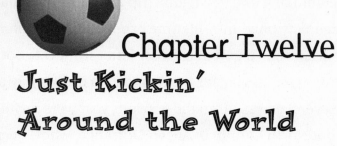

Chapter Twelve

Just Kickin'
Around the World

I graduated from the University of Central Florida following my final collegiate soccer season that fall semester of 1988. With my bachelor's degree in liberal studies and health, I still planned to pursue my long-time dream of becoming a paramedic. Eventually. But my immediate plan was to follow my heart, pursue my first love, and figure out some way I could afford to train and play soccer full-time.

There were no professional soccer teams for women. The U.S. women's soccer team didn't pay any of its players; we received ten dollars per day (for meals and expenses) the few days a year we got together. Fifteen dollars a day when traveling overseas. So money certainly wasn't the appeal. I just wanted to play soccer— to do what I loved doing most—for as long as I could. As a brand-new college graduate and a four-year veteran of the U.S. women's soccer team, I had already collected a wealth of memories.

After thinking that first team's trip to Italy in 1985 may have been my once-in-a-lifetime experience with international soccer, I'd gotten another letter from U.S. Soccer inviting me to play for the team again during July of 1986. Several players from the previous year were invited back, but North Carolina's Anson Dorrance, who'd been named our new coach, brought more college stars he'd known or coached. Our 5–2 record for 1986 reflected our gradual but definite improvement as a national team.

The U.S. Women's National Team played its most ambitious schedule yet in 1987. We hosted four games in Blaine, Minnesota, that summer: beating Canada, losing to Sweden, and splitting two games against a team from Norway. The team made its first trip to China in August for a two-game set against their national team. We won one game and tied the other.

I missed that trip with another injured knee, but during the December break between semesters I rejoined the team on a memorable ten-day, five-game trip to Taipai, Taiwan. We beat Japan 1–0 before losing to New Zealand by the same score. I scored one goal in a 6–0 rout of Australia and two more in our team's 4–0 defeat of Canada, prior to losing the final game of the series to Taiwan 1–2. But far more vivid than any detailed memories

I have from those games are the fascinating images I still recall from my very first exposure to the sights and sounds of the Far East.

❀ ❀ ❀

A 6–4–1 finish gave that team one more win than they'd managed the previous year. But the most note-worthy change in 1987 wasn't the record, the more exten-sive schedule, or the team's first two trips to the Orient. The most significant development was a decision Anson Dor-rance made that summer. When the national team played its invitational tournament in Minnesota in July, the U.S. junior national team was also there to play. Many of those under–19 players did so well that Anson told his national team that he was going with youth. He cut a number of veterans to make immediate room on the national team for "the youngsters": eighteen-year-olds Linda Hamilton, Joy Biefeld (Fawcett), and Carla Werden (Overbeck); Julie Foudy and Kristine Lilly, who were all of sixteen; and fif-teen-year-old Mia Hamm.

❀ ❀ ❀

While our new players all showed flashes of potential, I did think Foudy, Lil, and Mia in particular seemed pretty scrawny and a bit intimidated to begin with. They were just kids, young enough that they had to get parental permission to make those first overseas trips. And Lil still gets teased for taking along a raggedy stuffed tiger named Tamba because she couldn't sleep without him.

But if Anson wanted these changes and thought these kids could help the team, we'd go with them. As usual, my focus was playing soccer, not the team roster.

In June of 1988 I was injury-free and made my first trip to China for the first-ever Women's World Tournament sanctioned by FIFA, the Federation of International Football Associations. What an experience that turned out to be!

Every meal was a cross-cultural adventure. The head of our delegation told us that even though China was a poor country, they wanted to give us the best of everything they had. We begged for plain rice, but we were informed that rice was poor peoples' food; it wasn't good enough for special guests.

We didn't always know what we were eating. So we used veteran Lori Henry as our unofficial team taster. When a dish looked or smelled suspicious, we always waited for Lori to take the first bite. If she liked it and said, "It tastes just like chicken," most of us would take a chance.

But no sooner would we take our first tentative nibble than Lori or someone else would invariable give a little bark and we'd all groan in disgust. We probably did have dog at some point. I know we were served turtle soup, ox, snake, and, we suspected, cat. Sometimes the hardest things to eat were the ones we could identify all too easily. Like the time we had soup containing whole fish (including the heads) or the chicken dish served with the entire neck and head sticking out as garnish.

After graduation from college in 1988, to make ends meet and cover my very modest living expenses, I accepted an assistant coaching job with the women's soccer team at the University of Central Florida. A few months later, during the spring of 1989 I received an intriguing phone call.

The man on the other end of the line told me he was a sports agent. "How would you like to become the first woman to ever play in the National Football League?" he asked.

Is this guy serious? Me? Play in the NFL? Yeah, whatever, dude.

It turned out he was serious. He wanted to know, Could I come to Dallas to meet him for a tryout as a placekicker?

So I flew to Dallas and spent a few hours on a field giving the agent a kicking exhibition. I didn't know what to expect. I'd never kicked field goals before. *But how hard can it be?* Turns out it wasn't tough at all without any linemen trying to squash me into the turf. The agent seemed especially impressed when I kicked a fifty-two-yarder through the uprights.

The man told me he'd talked with a Dallas Cowboys special teams coach who would be conducting a kicking clinic soon near his home in Santa Barbara, California. So the agent and I flew to California. After seeing me kick a football, the coach told me he thought I definitely had the potential to play in the NFL. If I'd be willing to spend the next year working out to build up my strength and train full-time for football, he said, "You can make it!"

I thought about it. I figured he was probably right; I could do it. Kicking a football was fun. I might make history as the first woman to ever play in the NFL. But that would mean having to quit doing what I enjoyed doing more than anything else—which was playing *real* football.

"I'm sorry, but I'm not going to do this," I told the agent as he drove me back to the hotel. "What I really want is to be a world-class soccer player." He was so unhappy that he left me stranded at the hotel without a ride to the airport the next morning. I never saw the guy again.

When I injured my knee again, I missed the one and only game the national team played in 1989. A 0–0 tie with Poland in a game played in Sardinia, Italy.

With my collegiate career finished and no international competition at all, I spent 1989 trying to find ways to stay in training and keep soccer fit. Assistant coaching at UCF gave me contacts there in the men's and women's programs. I could work out along with those teams, and often find enough willing bodies for regular competitive pickup games. But once school let out and it got tougher to round up workout partners, I had to do a lot more on my own.

So in 1990 I left the country for three months to play for the Tyreso FF team in the Elite Division of a Swedish club league. I went because there were no comparable opportunities for ex-college players at the time in the United States. And because the Tyreso club promised to provide me with a place to stay and living expenses while I played.

❊ ❊ ❊

By the time Michelle rejoined her teammates on the national team at their Minnesota training camp in July of 1990, she had raised her game to a new level. She played not just with a vengeance—she'd always done that—but with a confidence no one had ever seen in her before.

She scored a goal in two of the three games played in Winnipeg, Canada, in which the U.S. defeated Norway (4–0), Canada (4–1), and Norway again (4–2). But the next week back in Blaine, Michelle had a break-out performance with seven goals in just three games against the USSR, England, and West Germany.

That was the entire 1990 schedule. Michelle had scored nine goals. The U.S. played only six games, winning them all. And none of the games were even close.

✿ ✿ ✿

After our final game of the year—when we defeated West Germany, a team many considered the world's top women's soccer team, by the surprising score of 3–0— Coach Dorrance gathered the team together in the locker room for one last speech. He congratulated us on our best performance ever as a team and our most successful season. He thanked us for the effort we'd made not only that summer, but over all the years leading up to that point. He reminded us of all we'd been through together.

Then Anson assured us he had it on good authority that plans were already in the works for the first Women's World Cup to be held in China sometime near the end of 1991. He told us such a tournament would be the fulfillment of a dream many people had worked for years to accomplish. He promised it would be unlike anything any of us had ever experienced. The pressure would be more intense, the competition stiffer, the challenge tougher than we had ever known before.

Even as Anson spoke we all knew full well what he was doing. He was a master motivator. He had the entire team hooked and hanging on his every word.

I proudly displayed my first trophy after a 1970 fishing expedition with my dad.

The only downside to my first day of school at Montague Elementary in Santa Clara, California, in the fall of 1972 was having to wear a dress.

Dad, Mom, Mike, and me at my grandparents' for Christmas.

I lettered in soccer all four years for the Shorecrest Scots. We won the state championship my senior year.

I wanted to quit my first soccer team, the Cougars, because I hated losing every game even more than I hated the team colors. Mom (top right) made me stick it out. I'm second from the right in the first row, in braids and my sweet pink uniform.

Here's a recent shot of me with Al Kovats, my fave high school teacher and a major influence on my life.

Dad flew clear across the country to watch me play a warm-up game against China prior to the 1991 World Cup. When I got booted (red carded) early in the match we had some unexpected together time in the stands.

My freshman college roommate and S.W.A.T. partner, Amy Allmann, also played with me on the Women's National Team. Here we are on a team trip to Bulgaria in 1991.

I played college soccer for the University of Central Florida in Orlando. That's me wearing #10, fourth from the left on the second row.

I scored the first goal versus Norway in the 1991 World Cup final on a header.

PHIL STEPHENS

With only minutes remaining in the final match, I
stole the ball en route to scoring the winning goal
in the 2-1 U.S. victory over Norway.

Yeah, baby! We did it! The first ever
Women's World Cup champs!

Hiking in the Cascades has always been my favorite getaway. Here I am with my brother, Mike, in 1993.

When I signed my very first endorsement deal in 1991, I was truly honored to have Pele there to welcome me into the Umbro family.

JUDY NELSON

I board my horse Vinnie on a farm outside Orlando and ride him every chance I get.

My family's cabin in the mountains outside Seattle has always been a favorite place for retreat and renewal.

After double knee surgery while playing pro in Sweden during 1994, the Swedish doctor told me my soccer playing days were over. I was too stubborn to listen.

Our team trainer, Patty Marchak, had to guide me off the field after a head-to-head collision with a Chinese player nearly ended my '95 World Cup experience in the opening minutes of the very first game.

I made it back to play one-legged in our 1-0 semifinal loss to Norway. This Akers sandwich shot pretty accurately shows what kind of game it was for me.

My penalty kick in the '96 Olympics tied the semifinal against Norway and sent the game into overtime. We won 2-1.

During the medal ceremony I had to search the stands for Dad.

When I spotted him I showed and shared the Gold Medal moment with my Pops.

Yes! Rock on! Putting the shot in the back of the net, knowing an Olympic medal was on the line, was one of the greatest feelings in the world!

Looking a little black and blue after breaking my face in yet another head-to-head collision in the FIFA World All-Star game in February of 1999.

Cool, huh! Four of my teammates and I became the first soccer players ever to make it on the Wheaties box.

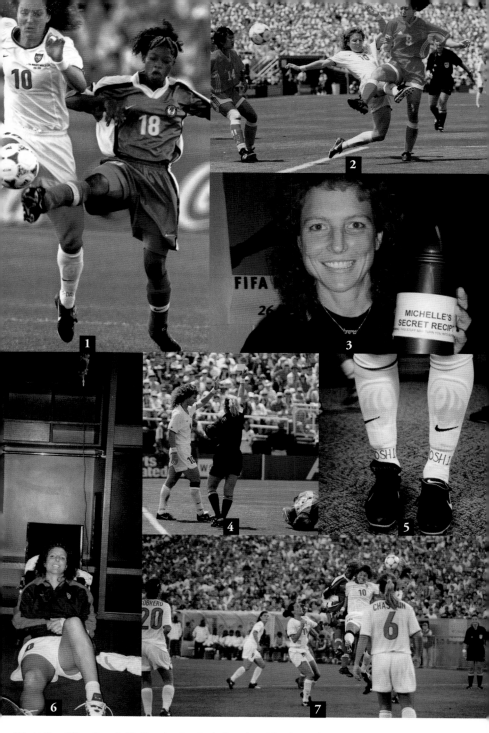

World Cup '99 action: 1. Challenging for the ball against Nigeria. 2. A tough tackle vs. China. 3. My extra special coffee brew helped raise my blood pressure enough to play. 4. Getting yellow carded for rough play during the final. 5. I wrote Joshua 1:9, my inspirational Bible verse, on my socks for the final. 6. My typical post-game IV treatment. 7. Winning a header against Nigeria.

1. Got my bell rung again. 2. Doc Adams takes me to the trauma room after I collapsed in the 90th minute in the final. 3. A little later I made it back out to celebrate. Number one, baby! 4. Smashing through a Denmark player to win a headball. 5. Celebrating my PK against Brazil in the semifinal game. 6. One very short victory lap for the crowd; one very special moment for me.

Anson raised our sights and our hopes by assuring us that the rewards would be worth everything it was going to cost us. And he finished his speech by declaring his vision and his goal. "I want this team to be the best in the world! Are you with me?"

Doggone right we were with him! Are you kidding?

We were so fired up we could have whipped the entire world right then and there.

My teammates and I accepted Anson's challenge. From that day on, our goal was to be the best women's soccer team in the world.

But I also had a personal goal. I wanted to be the best woman player in the world. Nothing less would do.

 Chapter Thirteen

Long Road to China

By the time our next training camp rolled around the next March, I was more than ready to hit the field with my old teammates and begin our quest to be the best women's soccer team in the world.

Anson assembled a bunch of veterans for that 1991 squad. Even those "youngsters" he had seen as the future of national women's soccer and snatched off the U.S. junior team—Joy Biefeld (Fawcett), Julie Foudy, Mia Hamm, Kristine Lilly, Carla Werden (Overbeck), and Linda Hamilton—had all played regularly for three or four seasons already.

We knew each other. We knew what our coaches expected. And we thought we knew what had to be done. But what we had yet to learn was just how different 1991 would be from any of the years that had come before. And the reason was the World Cup.

✦ ✦ ✦

The 1991 U.S. Women's National Team began its year
with a tune-up tour to Bulgaria where in the first eight
days of April they played and won five shutouts against
five different European national teams.

By scoring an amazing eight goals in those five games,
even though she came out of two games early, Michelle
established herself as the go-to player on the U.S. team.
Later that month Michelle easily won the qualifying tour-
nament MVP award, scoring an astounding eleven goals
in just five games. She tallied two goals apiece in the first
four games which turned into U.S. routs of Mexico (12–0),
Martinique (12–0), Trinidad and Tobago (10–0), and
Haiti (10–0). Then to top it all off, she netted three balls in
the 5–0 final against Canada to win the tournament and
clinch a spot in the World Cup later in the year.

✦ ✦ ✦

The more games we played that year the more I
noticed another attitude shift among my teammates. The
closer we got to that first Women's World Cup in 1991, the
longer we pursued our world championship goal, the
greater grew the sense that we weren't just playing soccer for ourselves, but for a greater purpose—a purpose
we all shared. Whether or not very many of our fellow cit-

izens yet realized it or cared, we were indeed representing friends, family, and country. We really were playing for the USA.

And that gave our team an unprecedented sense of mission, resolve, and unity. It was now *us* against the world!

Soon after we returned from our second European trip of the year, I got a phone call from Mick Hoban, an Umbro executive, who wanted to fly me to the company's annual sales meeting for a banquet where I would sign a contract to represent his company and endorse their soccer apparel. This was a big deal—not just for me but for the sport. Never before had any company signed a woman soccer player to an endorsement contract.

The banquet itself turned out to be a very impressive affair—with a wonderful surprise in my honor. I sat up front where I was introduced to all the Umbro folks and their guests. And then after dinner the lights went down and a voice boomed out over the speakers: "When Michelle Akers was still a little girl kicking a ball around her backyard in Santa Clara, California, Brazilian soccer superstar Pelé . . . the greatest soccer player in the history of the world . . . was leading his nation's teams to World Cup glory . . . playing for the New York Cosmos in this country's first professional soccer league. . . ."

At the same time, footage of Pelé playing and scoring and celebrating his many triumphs was being projected on a giant screen behind me. Then the film ended, the lights came back up—and there on the platform, smiling and waving in acknowledgment of the applause and cheers of our audience, stood Pelé himself. As a long-time company spokesperson, he welcomed me into the Umbro family and presented me with one of his Cosmos jerseys which he autographed to me on the spot.

I was so overwhelmed, it was all I could do to keep my bottom jaw from falling to the floor. Here I was sharing a platform with the great Pelé. I couldn't believe it. I chatted a while that evening with Pelé, telling him about our team and asking him about his World Cup experience. What a warm, wonderful man.

And I did agree to represent Umbro, though I had no idea at the time what that would involve. I remember being excited about the prospect of having enough income that I could afford to keep playing soccer and not have to borrow money to cover my expenses while I trained for the national team.

I knew this was an important first not just for me but for women's soccer. So I proudly signed my name to that endorsement contract thinking, *Good! People are starting to notice us. Now all the other players on the team will get sponsors of their own.*

But that didn't happen right way. And in the meantime I still had to prepare for my own first World Cup.

In August of 1991, during a short break in our national team schedule, I worked for a week at a soccer camp in California. I was out on the field doing a breakaway demo. On a long touch toward goal, as I tried to get past the goalkeeper, he dove, stuffing me and the ball. I went sailing over the top and when I hit the ground I heard a CLUNK. I had landed on a sprinkler head sticking out of the turf. I remember thinking, *Uh, oh! This could be bad.* I rolled over Bernie, the keeper, and got a good look at my right knee. The metal had torn a wicked-looking gash so deep and so long that it looked like I'd sliced my kneecap halfway off. I quickly pulled a chunk of loose sod out of the wound and covered it with my hand so no one else would freak out if they saw it. Bernie yelled for help. Thankfully there was a trainer on site who helped carry me off the field and sat with me on the sideline applying pressure to control the bleeding until the session ended. Then we went to a local emergency room where a San Diego Chargers doctor used sixty-some stitches to sew everything back together.

He also told me I shouldn't be walking on that knee for a while. That it would be weeks, maybe months, before I should start playing on it again. That I might even have to miss the World Cup. I remember thinking, *We'll see about that!*

Then I had to place a very difficult call to Anson telling him what had happened. "I don't know how long it will be before I can play," I said. Then I had to hang up on him and run on my crutches to the bathroom and throw up because the pain medication was tearing up my stomach.

But what bothered me even more was knowing I'd be facing the most important games of my life that fall at less than a hundred percent.

Chapter Fourteen
World Cup Glory

In the last weeks before the World Cup I spent a lot of time trying to imagine what the experience would be like. In my mind I had this recurring vision that always ended the same way:

I leaped into the air with my arms extended in victory. And as my feet hit the ground, I sprinted wildly toward my teammates. Weak with exhaustion and emotion, I saw happy, smiling faces. Some crying. Others laughing. Many doing both at the same time.

We hugged and tackled each other, rolling around on the ground. We were celebrating the first world championship of women's soccer. And when we regained our composure, we lined up to accept the trophy before our families and sixty thousand applauding fans.

Every time a different ending to my World Cup dream entered my thoughts, I immediately dismissed it. In my mind only a fairy-tale ending would do.

✵ ✵ ✵

Sixteen thousand fans packed the stadium in Punyu, China, for our opening game against Sweden. *Amazing.* I don't know that we'd ever played in front of that many people in any one year, let alone one game. *What a feeling!*

Before the game the national anthem brought tears to my eyes. It hit me like a wave. I realized, *This is it!* The anticipation of the unknown—victory or defeat—was almost too much for me.

No matter how much nervous energy and adrenaline is pumping before a game, once the action begins and my body gets a little tired, I lose the nervous edge and begin to feel more composed. Once I focus, it's as if everything shifts into slow motion and I can almost see things develop before they happen. But through the entire game against Sweden everything seemed to be racing at a hundred miles an hour. It never slowed down.

Carin Jennings tallied two goals early. So when Mia Hamm scored on a twenty-five-yarder during the 61st minute to give us a 3–0 lead, the game looked to be over. But Sweden scored twice in the next 10 minutes and we staggered around in exhaustion the last 20 minutes of the game, fighting desperately to hang on. When the final whistle sounded we hadn't so much *won* as we had *survived*, 3–2.

We determined not to make the same mistake against Brazil on Tuesday. We didn't. April scored two goals. Carin, Mia, and I each scored one in what turned out to be a much-easier-than-expected 5–0 win in our first-ever encounter with Brazil. Since the top two teams from each of three groupings, plus the two second-place teams with the best records, all advanced, we knew we'd already qualified for the quarterfinals. So Anson took the opportunity against Japan to rest five of our starters who were banged up with various dings and bruises. I scored early in the game to give us the lead. Then I scored again and Wendy Gebauer slotted our third and final score just before the half in a game that never seemed in doubt.

✥ ✥ ✥

In the opening round games of the World Cup, after each of the three top scorers on the U.S. national team had contributed two-goal games, the Chinese press dubbed the offensive line of Heinrichs, Jennings, and Akers the American's dangerous "three-edged sword." A fortunate opponent might avoid one or two, but never all three.

What admiring press and fans didn't know was, they hadn't seen anything yet. In the quarterfinals, Michelle did much better than "well." She set a World Cup record (which still stands) with an astounding five goals in her team's 7–0 trouncing of Taiwan.

✿ ✿ ✿

After playing our first four games in the cities of Punyu and Foshan, we were back in Guangzhou, the official World Cup city, for the remainder of the tournament. That had been a major goal since our arrival in China. Not only because it meant that we'd advanced to the final rounds, but because we were now finally staying in a first-class hotel which actually served American hamburgers.

We all had fire in our eyes when we paraded into Guangzhou's Tianhe Stadium for our match with Germany. From the start of the game it was clear the Germans had determined they were not going to let me beat them. Fortunately, I didn't have to. I'd never taken the kind of physical pounding I received in that game. Fouled repeatedly and absolutely hammered a number of times, I could only get back up and continue to distribute the ball to the other two edges of our "three-edged sword" attack. April scored twice and Gumby (our team's name for Carin because she was pigeon-toed and so deceptive with her dribbling skills that her crazy legs whipped back and forth like rubber when she dribbled down the field) netted three balls.

By the time the final whistle blew for a final score of 5–2, I collapsed in exhaustion and cried in relief. We had made the finals!

The next day was Thanksgiving. And there was so much for which we were grateful, not the least of which was a traditional American holiday feast, complete with turkey, dressing, and all the trimmings, which hadn't been that easy to come by in China.

Our team administrator, Heather Kashner, who arranged our special meal, had first asked our hosts if they could get us some turkeys for a holiday dinner. She got back to our hotel the next night to find a flock of live turkeys in her hotel room—like we were going to kill them, pluck them, clean them, and cook them ourselves. She had to graciously return the birds to our hosts, explaining that we preferred frozen Butterballs. Once we sorted out that little cross-cultural misunderstanding, our Thanksgiving dinner turned out to be yet another incredible memory for us to share with our parents and families.

Contrary to what most people might think, I felt surprisingly relaxed going into the final. But it was hard to think of anything else for the next two days. We were now only one step away from our dream.

Walking into the stadium for the final I looked for my family. Even among more than sixty-five thousand Chinese—the largest crowd that had ever witnessed any women's sporting event to that time—I spotted Dad right away. He waved wildly. So I gave him a big thumbs-up gesture—which has been our personal tradition at soccer games ever since—and thought again how wonderful it was to have family behind us.

Sixty-five thousand people! Unbelievable! We'd played international games with crowds so small the fans couldn't have joined hands and stretched all the way around the field once. Now here we were playing in a packed-out stadium with our families present to enjoy the game and the glory.

When the game finally started, the Norwegians came out fired up. But so did we.

Twenty minutes into the contest the official awarded us a free kick just outside the penalty box, twenty-five to thirty yards from the goal on the right side. Shannon Higgins lofted a beauty, high toward the net. I leaped along with a Norwegian girl at the front edge of the six-yard keeper box, got my head on the ball, and sent it sailing back to the goalkeeper's left and into the right side of the net for our first score.

Unfortunately that lead didn't last long. Norway scored minutes later off a free kick of their own. For the rest of the first half we ran up and down the field with neither team getting an advantage or capitalizing on any scoring chances.

We took a 1–1 tie into our halftime locker room. I remember sitting there, not listening to anything the coaches said, just wanting to get back out on the field and play.

Traipsing out the tunnel for the second half, Tony DiCicco, our goalkeeper coach at the time, walked beside me. "Mish," he said, "you're going to be the one. You're going to have to take control of this game yourself."

I nodded. "Okay, Tony. Okay."

And that's what I set out to do. But the second half started much like the first. The Norwegians banged long balls into our half with our defenders trying to the clear balls out before they could press the advantage. Every time we'd work the ball forward they'd whack it down-field over our midfielders and we'd have to turn and sprint back on defense again.

We were slowly wearing each other down, yet neither team could score. Most people were beginning to assume overtime or penalty kicks were inevitable. But I never quit feeling as if a chance would come.

With 5 minutes left in the game it happened. Shannon Higgins hit a long ball upfield. While it was a bit ahead of me, you never know what will happen if you apply a little pressure. So I sprinted after it. Two Norwegian defenders closed on the ball as it rolled toward their goal. And then they hesitated for a fraction of a second. Their mistake.

I picked up my speed and smashed into the girl closest to me, knocking her into her teammate. Before they could recover, the ball was mine.

I took a long touch a little to the left of the goal, and we had a footrace to see who would get to the ball first—the charging goalkeeper or me. I managed to touch the ball again to the left and still leap over the late-diving keeper. Suddenly there was no one between me and a wide-open goal.

I was a little wide to the left, so a thousand thoughts raced through my mind in the next split second. *Relax! This is my one chance. I've gotta make this. Don't kick it into the side netting. Don't kick it over. Whatever you do, don't miss the goal.* So I took one extra touch and passed it gently into the goal with the side of my right foot. USA 2, Norway 1.

We spent the rest of the game just trying to clear the ball out of the stadium. And when the final whistle blew, the celebration was just as I had imagined. I jumped. We hugged. We laughed and we cried. My screaming team-mates and I ran around in a wild frenzy, not knowing who to hug next or what to say. It was awesome. Even now, looking back, my memory of that celebration and the medal ceremony is one big crazy blur.

The American fans in the stands were going berserk at the same time. I spotted Dad waving wildly. Many parents and families found their way into our locker room where we shared more hugs and posed for laughing, teary photos clinging to one another and our world championship trophy.

Carin Jennings, who'd had such a fantastic tournament, won the Golden Ball Award as the tournament's Most Valuable Player. I was awarded the Golden Boot Award for scoring the most goals in the tournament—a total of ten in six games.

Julie Foudy may have summed up all our sentiments best by saying, "When we first started this team, we never thought there would be a world championship for women. It was always this mystical thing—a World Cup. And now we're holding it in our hands!"

The fairy-tale ending had come true. Just like I'd dreamed it would.

But if I thought that meant everyone was going to live happily ever after, I had never been more wrong.

Chapter Fifteen

Sidelined

Now that I'd achieved my dream, I expected life to be different. But I didn't really know how.

⚽ ⚽ ⚽

Her amazing ten-goal World Cup scoring record and her even more astounding total of thirty-nine goals in the twenty-six international games she played in 1991 had earned Michelle superstar status throughout the soccer world. And the following month she found herself representing Umbro as a featured speaker at the National Soccer Coaches Association of America convention.

⚽ ⚽ ⚽

I appreciated the respect being shown me in the soccer community. Being recognized for being good at what

I did was gratifying. But it felt strange to see people standing in line for my autograph.

It all seemed to happen so fast. A little over a month after the World Cup ended I felt like I had been placed on a pedestal and was now expected to be this outgoing personality who smiles and poses with fans and stands on a stage in front of thousands of people to tell them how to be "great." Sure I played soccer and was good at it. But suddenly I was also considered a role model. I didn't ask for that job, had never thought about it before, and certainly didn't know how to do it.

Only gradually did I begin to see what was happening as an important opportunity. It amazed and humbled me whenever I made some appearance, gave a presentation, or just signed autographs. I saw kids' eyes light up. I saw them dreaming. I saw people thinking twice about women's soccer. The media that never cared before suddenly swarmed around and asked questions. Every day, every appearance I made I felt was helpful for the U.S. soccer program.

As I came to appreciate this unprecedented platform I'd been given, I also realized that with any platform comes responsibility. Since I'm such a goal-oriented person, I very quickly identified and developed several worthy goals to pursue.

In addition to benefiting my national team and teammates, I determined to use my new platform to build and promote women's soccer in general. Because my profile was even higher in the international soccer community and countries with a longer and richer soccer heritage than the United States, FIFA sent me around the world to meet with other national federations and promote the women's game.

Those experiences provided me the contacts and the opportunities to work for yet another longtime personal goal. I joined what became a long, hard crusade to convince the International and U.S. Olympic Committees that women's soccer should be a medal sport in the 1996 summer games. I spoke out for the cause wherever I went, distributing petitions, and encouraging participants and fans of women's soccer to make their voices heard.

Since childhood I'd dreamed of what it would be like to compete for and win an Olympic gold medal. But whenever I'd casually mention it to friends or teammates they would always say things like, "Dream on, Michelle! Women's soccer isn't even an Olympic sport!" Now I wanted to help make it one.

The third objective I had was to use my platform to inspire and challenge those who were now looking up to me. I wanted all the kids who came to my clinics, who read my regular column in *Soccer Junior* magazine, who lined up for my autograph, to learn what I believed: If you want anything badly enough and you're willing to commit everything to work for that goal, you can succeed. I wanted to empower people to pursue and achieve their greatest dreams. In other words, I intended to change the world—through soccer.

While speaking for and promoting an entire sport seemed an overwhelming job at times, I determined to give it my all. However, as I tried to be everywhere and do everything for everyone else, I forgot about taking care of myself.

At the same time my soccer success brought all these exciting opportunities in my professional life, my own physical health started on a steep and steady decline. I came home from the 1991 World Cup feeling absolutely exhausted. I figured that feeling would go away once life settled back to normal, the demand of all the public appearances slowed down, and I could finally get enough rest and sleep. But as time went by, I became increasingly listless and achy, like I was engaged in a never-ending battle with the flu. Over time I felt noticeably worse, not better. I began to feel dizzy. I suffered frequent migraine headaches, nausea, and could never seem to get enough sleep.

Finally I went to the doctor.

"You need to take it easy," he said. "You had the World Cup last year. Now all this travel and appearance business. You just need a vacation."

I figured he was probably right. So I took things a little easier for a couple months before I jetted off to Sweden to play the 1992 soccer season with my old professional team. I lived for the season in an apartment in what was actually an ancient Swedish castle—picturesque accommodations, though a bit cool and drafty, which were generously provided by one of the board members of the Tyreso football club.

I still didn't feel right physically. Where I'd always been such a high-energy person, something inside me was definitely changing. I slept twelve hours a night and still needed a two-hour nap in the afternoons. I pushed myself to keep playing soccer. And I performed well enough to win the *Canon Shot Award,* given to the top goal scorer in Sweden's men's and women's club leagues, for the 1992 season. Yet I could feel my strength fading as the months rolled by.

Fortunately for me, since I was struggling with my health, it just so happened that the national team didn't have much of a schedule the year after our World Cup triumph. In all of 1992 we played just two games—against Norway—up in New England the middle of August.

Unfortunately for me, time and rest didn't work to improve my physical condition at all.

My doctor finally diagnosed me with a severe case of mononucleosis. That gave me hope. And something I could explain. The only cure for mono was time and more rest—which is what I tried.

By 1993, I would often sweat through two or three T-shirts a night and wake up the next morning feeling like I'd flown to Europe overnight without food or sleep, gotten right back on a return flight to the States, landed, and gone straight to soccer practice. Some days I felt so bad I couldn't sit up in a chair. The racking migraines stranded me at home alone, unable even to get up and brush my teeth or find something to eat. Just surviving through the day seemed like an accomplishment.

I pushed myself to make a trip with the national team to Cyprus in March and even scored a goal in a 2–0 win over Denmark in our opener. But I struggled just to finish the game in 0–1 losses to Norway and Germany. I spent most of the trip in bed, blowing my nose, hacking away, and trying in vain to get a good night's sleep.

I scored three goals as the team won five of six international games we played back in the States throughout the spring. But I remained so weak I couldn't even finish three of those matches. I skipped an entire five-game tournament held in Canada early that summer.

During this time I didn't tell the coaches or my teammates how I was really feeling or what was going on, in large part because I didn't know what to tell them. Also I figured if I could psych myself up enough to stay on my feet just long enough to practice or contribute something in a game, then I could go to bed and crash afterwards and no one needed to know.

The strategy worked until the Olympic Sports Festival in San Antonio that July.

I became so delirious during a game that I wandered off the field in the wrong direction. My teammates had to come and get me.

I stayed sick with a pounding migraine, utter exhaustion, and nausea for two days before I tried to play again. I don't remember much at all from that game except feeling disoriented—like I was drunk or something—before I completely passed out on the field.

⚽ ⚽ ⚽

"I saw her go down on the field in San Antonio," Anson Dorrance recalls. *"No one hit her. She wasn't even in on a play. She seemed fine one second. Then she passed out and had to be carried off the field.*

"Michelle's dad and I were with her in the medical tent when she came to with a pained and confused look in her eyes. I remember holding a cool wet cloth against her forehead and not knowing what to say when she asked, 'What happened?' Frankly I was scared."

No one knew what to say or think because no one knew what could be wrong. A lot of people were scared for her.

⚽ ⚽ ⚽

Including me.

 ## Chapter Sixteen

Down from the Mountain Top

I took things easy again for a week or so, until I started to feel a little better—and began training once more. Bam! I was sick again.

As frustrating as my health struggles had been over the two years since the '91 World Cup, they hadn't yet seriously hampered my soccer career. Primarily because the national team hadn't played any significant games during that time. But I knew 1994 would be different. The U.S. women's team once again had a slate of matches scheduled to begin gearing up for the next Women's World Cup to be held in Sweden in 1995.

If I was going to help lead my team to another world championship, I needed to be healthy. I needed answers. And fast.

That's when I went back to my doctor in Orlando, and tested positive for chronic Epstein-Barr Virus (EBV)—which I understood as a more serious form of mono. It is also referred to as Chronic Fatigue Dysfunction Syndrome. I didn't know exactly what that meant. But the *fatigue* part sounded accurate enough. Hopefully the doctor was right this time.

He told me to rest up, alter my schedule a bit, and my body should bounce back and overcome the virus in six to eight months or so. I decided to shorten my training a bit, and tried to maintain as much of my schedule as possible in the meantime. In March I joined the team for a training camp and a trip to Portugal to play in the Algarve Cup tournament. We won two games before losing to Norway in the final 0–1. I was sick, battling yet another chest cold. So I only played a few minutes in each of the three games and didn't score a goal the entire tournament. *But at least I played. Slow, steady progress.*

We played three more games in Trinidad and Tobago a few weeks later. I only lasted a few minutes in two of them. But I did score three goals. *More progress.*

I went to Sweden right after that for the beginning of the Tyreso club season. I figured my familiarity with the Swedish league made that a good place to keep playing and making as much progress as I could.

❁ ❁ ❁

Three of Michelle's U.S. teammates joined her on the Tyreso club that year. Julie Foudy, Kristine Lilly, and Mary

Harvey all decided that a few weeks of competitive Swedish soccer would keep them tuned up until the national team schedule resumed that summer.

Michelle enjoyed the camaraderie. And her friends' presence certainly made for a better Tyreso team. But being together every day for such a long stretch of time made it impossible for Michelle to keep hiding how much she was struggling.

"Obviously something was wrong," says Julie Foudy. "We would train and then Michelle would go back home and chill out the rest of the day. All she did the whole time we were there was play soccer and sleep. She never seemed to have any energy to do anything else."

⚽ ⚽ ⚽

Back home that summer I began working out with a new training partner. Steve Slain was a strength coach who worked for the Orlando Magic for several years and had trained a lot of professional athletes. After someone recommended him to me, we quickly struck up a friendship. He reminded me a lot of Mr. Kovats—kind and gentle. Steve, too, acted excited about his relationship with God. He studied the Bible on his own and got fired up about going to church.

For the past few years I'd pretty much forgotten about being a Christian. Yet I think deep down I'd realized something was missing in my life spiritually. Being around Steve reminded me.

Physically, my immediate goal was to work my way up to playing a full 90-minute game. But that didn't happen right away.

In August we flew to Montreal to begin the qualifying tournament to see who would represent our region at the World Cup in Sweden the following year. I started every game and scored a total of six goals for the tournament. But I didn't finish a single match. Fortunately the team didn't need me since we outscored our regional opponents by an overwhelming margin of 36 goals to 1.

As far as I was concerned, the only good thing about the tournament was that we'd won. We were now qualified for the '95 World Cup in Sweden the following June.

When the tournament ended, I decided to go out to my family's mountain cabin in the Cascades outside of Seattle. After all the pain and discouragement I'd been through, I needed a place near my family to sort out my feelings and think about my life, my health, my future.

Just arriving at the cabin, a place filled with peace and solitude, seemed to soothe my soul. Mountains, rivers, and nature always had a way of humbling and inspiring me. I needed that—now more than ever.

My second day at the cabin, I set out on a short hike through the woods and was feeling so good I'd walked sixteen miles through the mountains before I realized it and had to hurry—sprinting the last two hundred yards—to get back before dark.

I paid for that adventure the next day, and the day after that, when I felt so sick I could do nothing but lie on the couch and try to recover my strength. I realized then that a change of scenery alone wouldn't cure me.

I stayed so sick over the remainder of my stay that a five-minute walk wiped me out for the day. I was forced to spend most of my time at the cabin sitting and thinking about who I was.

I honestly didn't know. And that scared me.

Epstein-Barr, CFIDs, or whatever you wanted to call this illness I'd been fighting, was a thief—yanking, grabbing, and systematically stealing everything that had been important to me. My health. My physical strength. My soccer career. My independence. My identity.

All that was gone. I didn't know where. And I had no idea how to go about getting it back.

There was this huge hole in my life and nothing to fill it with.

I couldn't have put it into words at the time, but the feeling reminded me of the emptiness and despair I'd felt as a teenager. And I remembered the incredible, indescribable peace that had come when I made my decision to give my life to God. *I want that again,* I thought. And in that instant I realized I needed to get things right with God.

Being around Steve Slain had reminded me I hadn't spent much time thinking about spiritual things since high school after Mr. Kovats introduced me to his faith in Christ. I'd gone to church a few times, mostly on Easter and Christmas, over the past few years. But my beliefs really didn't have anything to do with my daily life or my soccer career. I'd thrown up a prayer now and again for help or strength or a team win. But I always made my own decisions and dealt with the consequences. And all in all, I thought I'd done a pretty good job of keeping things under control.

Until now.

Now, as I sat in that cabin with nothing to do but examine my life, I didn't like what I saw. And I couldn't imagine where to go from here.

That was when I received a package Steve Slain sent me—tapes from a series of sermons his minister had recently preached. The first cassette I popped into my Walkman was a sermon about how easy it is for Christians to let new experiences and relationships crowd out their love of Jesus, how they can lose the closeness they once felt toward God.

As I listened to that tape there in the Cascades, the words hit home. Alone in the mountains, examining my life and my heart, I realized that was exactly what had happened with me. I had forsaken God for years. I had let other relationships and other things come between us.

"You can have all this stuff," I told God. "You can have this body. You can have this life. You can have me. Because I've made a mess of everything."

I finally came down out of the mountains to visit my family in Seattle. And on a Sunday I went to church with my grandparents.

In his sermon their minister told the story of a family God called to go to Africa as missionaries. He talked about what it means to be chosen and how God gives everyone special talents they can use to let others know about Him.

Once again I felt as if a preacher was speaking directly to me. I tried to ignore him. But I got this vision in my mind as clear as the dream I'd once had of us winning and celebrating the world championship in China. Instead of jumping up and down and running around a soccer field, this time I saw myself speaking to churches and soccer groups around the world—not just about soccer, but about Jesus.

I knew up in the mountains a few days earlier I'd told God He could have me. But I hadn't expected this. So right there in church I tried arguing with God: "Why me? Why do You have to pick me? I want to be a normal person in one area of my life and now You want to make me different in that area, too."

The idea upset me so badly I walked out before the minister even finished his sermon. I just whispered to my grandma that I had to leave, and I stood up and practically ran out of that church. I found a pay phone a couple blocks away and immediately called Steve Slain in Orlando.

When he answered, I practically shouted at him: "Slainer, you're not gonna believe what just happened to me!"

He assured me that if this was what God was calling me to do, then God would give me whatever it took to do it. Maybe he was right. After all, I'd spent the last few years learning how to stand up in front of all kinds of audiences to talk about soccer. Maybe that was all preparation for this. Maybe.

But the thought of being some kind of missionary still scared me to death. *Me? A missionary for Jesus? This is just too much!*

Chapter Seventeen

Looking up Again

Ireturned to Florida from Seattle that fall with a renewed spirit. I still experienced up and down emotions. My health wavered as well. But my heart felt new.

I hired Steve Slain as a personal trainer and began working out with him five days a week. Over time I began to sense a little of that inner, spiritual peace I'd felt as a teenager. But I still wasn't sure how to cultivate a relationship with God. So Steve helped with my spiritual training as well, telling me that if I wanted to grow spiritually I needed to be fed. And if God did want to use me to reach out to others—a prospect I still wasn't so sure about—I first needed the kind of nourishment and strengthening that he had found through his church and a weekly program called Bible Study Fellowship. So I started attending Northland Community Church with Steve on Sundays and signed up for BSF during the week.

Northland Community Church wasn't like most churches I'd ever attended. It met in a remodeled roller rink—which seemed kinda cool. I also really liked feeling I didn't have to dress up. And the music was great. At first I didn't know what to think about the preacher, though. He talked a lot about the importance of including God in our lives—in all our plans and all our relationships. It was like this minister, Joel Hunter, had an inside line to my heart and was preaching his sermons every week right at me.

When I mentioned it to Steve, he laughed and told me he'd felt the same way when he'd first visited Northland. And that God still often used the words of the pastor's sermons to speak directly to him.

Whatever the explanation, I felt an inner strength and hope that wasn't there before. And I started to put my life back together.

Another encouraging development came along in December when the U.S. Soccer Federation, for the first time ever, offered contracts to a number of veteran players so we could actually make a living while we trained. All this promised to make life a little easier for everyone as we prepared for the next summer's world championship.

In a way, training and working out made me feel better. On the other hand, it made me feel worse. When I could do it I enjoyed being outside in the fresh air—playing soccer, being physical, challenging myself. I was with the team, my friends, so I was not alone in my misery. At the same time it was tough to deal with mentally because I realized I still couldn't train as hard as I wanted or needed to.

Neither my mind nor my body were responding the way they had in the past. Even at my best I felt sluggish, tired, slow. I was not the same player. I had no endurance. I wasn't fit. And that really frustrated me.

Now when my mind said "yes," my body would say "no way!"

The work with Slainer and the time spent with my teammates in residency camp only gradually began to pay off. When I played my first full game in almost two years against Denmark in February, I was more excited over finishing the game than I was about scoring three goals.

Throughout this time, my renewed faith was at the center of my recovery. Despite my physical ups and downs I was happier most of the time. I had begun to accept the idea that maybe God did have a specific plan for my life.

I really did want to put my life in His hands. But I was so used to doing things on my own, my own way, that it wasn't easy. Where some people need a tap on the shoulder from God to get their attention, I think it required a two-by-four over the head to get through to me. The real message was, "Pay attention here, Michelle. This is important. You can't beat this on your own the way you've always managed everything else. You're going to have to rely on Me and I will give you what you need."

⚽ ⚽ ⚽

Michelle went with the team to Portugal to play in the Algarve Cup. Though the team struggled in Portugal with two wins and two losses, Michelle was encouraged by her own progress. She played all 90 minutes in the last two games and scored once. Yet again she paid a steep price— not just with her illness, but as a target for opponents who knew her reputation and roughed her up repeatedly to stop her. She returned to Florida from Portugal with a slight meniscus tear in her right knee, a shin hematoma, a deep thigh bruise, and a painful hip injury. Despite the battering, she was further encouraged when a visit to the doctor revealed her EBV numbers were way down.

⚽ ⚽ ⚽

After a quick three-game jaunt to France the middle of April it was home again for final World Cup preparations. I couldn't wait. My April 20 journal entry reveals my mood:

I looked at my photo albums yesterday. I decided to keep the 1991 World Cup one out to remind me of where I want to be and how hard it was to get there. I want to be a world champion again.

Spiritually, as well as physically, I still had a ways to go. But some progress was noted in my journal a few days later when I wrote:

There was a great service at church . . . on praying—when and how to do it. Joel Hunter, our preacher dude, was saying that God is not a "tooth fairy God," meaning you don't put your problems under your pillow and expect Him to magically take them away.

Yet that's exactly what I do.

I need to understand that God is giving me nothing I can't handle, and He gives me the means to get through it. He will bless me with something better (something a thousand times better than I can imagine if only I stay faithful). Just because He doesn't take my problems from me right now, it doesn't mean He's not listening. I can't give up. I have to keep praying and be thankful.

I had no idea how this lesson was about to be tested. When we arrived in Sweden on June 1, I wrote in my journal:

The team looks and feels ready. There's a quiet con-fidence. Less giddiness than in '91, more experience and calmness now. We'll just have to wait and see what comes up.

. . . This time when I try to envision the outcome it flashes between victory—sinking to my knees in relief and happiness, running crazy around the field, hugging everyone, and crying. Or . . . walking off the field with such an awful feeling in the pit of my stomach and wanting to punch each player on the other team as they celebrate what we wanted so badly.

I wonder which will happen. . . .

Chapter Eighteen
A Bitter Cup

felt the familiar spine-tingling excitement when we marched onto the field for the opening ceremonies of the 1995 Women's World Cup. As usual I looked for Dad, who was harder to find in a Swedish crowd than he had been in China. Fortunately that challenge was made easier by the fact that he was surrounded by a dozen relatives and friends who'd spent a small fortune to make the trip to watch me play my second World Cup.

When we finally kicked off, I thought, *Thank God! I'm at the World Cup again. I made it. Here we go.*

I think I got a total of two or three touches in the first 4 minutes of the game, before I dropped back to the edge of my own box to defend against a Chinese corner kick. The ball came in high. I jumped to head it away. I remember making contact and . . . the lights went out.

✿ ✿ ✿

As Michelle leaped into the air, a Chinese player's head speared hers at the base of the skull. Michelle's head snapped forward and she crumpled to the ground with her leg twisted under her at an awkward angle.

Ironically, Amy Allmann, Michelle's college roommate and former teammate on the national team, was doing color commentary on the game for ESPN2. "It was my job to describe the replays," Amy says. "When they showed the replay of Michelle's injury, I couldn't say a word. I was thinking, 'I hope Mish isn't paralyzed.'"

For a long time Michelle didn't move. When she returned to consciousness the team doctors took her to a nearby hospital where the diagnosis was a concussion and yet another knee injury.

Michelle slept for nearly twenty-four hours straight when she came back to the hotel from the hospital.

By the third day after the injury she'd recovered enough to write in her journal:

> So it's two games into the World Cup and I have played less than 6 minutes. Doc Garrett says I got over the Epstein-Barr only to get the Shanghai Shaft. Funny. Yeah, real funny. I had to go to the hospital for a CAT scan (yes, I have a brain)....
>
> Anyway, headwise I'm okay. But the knee is painful. A sprain to the right medial collateral ligament from the

> way I fell.... I'm hoping to be back in time for the
> quarterfinals next Tuesday.
>   Please, God!

The hardest part was facing my family and convincing them I was okay with it. Dad and Sue were so disappointed and sad for me that it hurt to see them. They'd flown halfway around the world to share another great experience with me and they'd only gotten to see me play for 6 minutes. I wanted everything to be okay for their sakes. And I couldn't help thinking, *What else am I going to put them through?*

I struggled at first with my role on the bench. As a career starter, it was tough sitting on the sideline watching. Good thing I was wearing sunglasses when our team doctor came over and told me I was handling it like a champion; I almost cried. People may have thought I had it all under control, but my disappointment remained very close to the surface. Only God gave me the strength and grace to get through it.

Yet I still hoped to get back into action before the tournament ended.

⚽ ⚽ ⚽

Michelle rehabbed her knee furiously. She could run a little as long as she moved in a straight line. Cutting caused excruciating pain. Kicking remained a problem as well.

"She'd make me go with her to a little patch of grass across the street from our hotel," her friend and roommate Amanda Cromwell recalls. "And we'd kick a ball back and forth. Every time her foot made contact she'd wince or cry out. Still she kept trying."

Even without Michelle in the lineup, her team advanced to the second round. Michelle hoped to come back by then. And on June 15, the day of the semifinal match with Norway, this is what she wrote in her journal:

> I start tonight, and for the first time ever, I'm terrified to play. I don't know what I will be able to do. My knee is sore from only thirty minutes of light running yesterday. What will it be like after an intense forty-five? Tony [DiCicco who had replaced Anson Dorrance as coach] says he doesn't expect me to "fly in and rescue the team," but I think a lot of people do. I just want to make a small difference. Actually, that's a lie. I want to make a huge difference. I want to score goals, be a threat, be the best player out on that field. And it's killing me knowing I won't be that player.

Norway scored a goal early and we spent the rest of the afternoon pounding shots at the Norwegian net, trying to fight back and tie. I limped around the field on one leg the entire game, unable to make anything good happen. I did what I could. But my best wasn't enough to make any difference that day.

When the final whistle blew I remember thinking three things. *This can't be real. I want another chance.* And *I refuse to let them see me cry.* The last thing in the world I wanted was to see my picture in some soccer magazine with tears streaming down my face.

So I just stood there, willing myself not to cry. I remember watching the Norwegians celebrating by forming a train and chugging happily around us on the field. It was awful shaking their hands. I felt more like punching them.

I headed toward the section of the stands where my family had been sitting. For some reason I was the only player who did. When the whole U.S. contingent of families and friends saw me coming, they started cheering. I couldn't look at them. I kept my head down until I got to my dad. Then I hugged him and began to cry. He cried. Sue cried. My brother cried. My grandmother cried. Everybody cried.

This was more than just another lost soccer match. They'd been through so much with me just to get there. And now we'd come up short.

Afterwards in my journal I wrote:

> Tony said some good stuff on the bus ride back to our hotel after the awards banquet. He said, "Never forget the feeling we have this night. The margin of victory on the field is so small. But the margin off the field is huge."

The Norwegians were in the limelight, receiving awards, holding the trophy. The U.S. in the back of the banquet room, unnoticed and forgotten. Hopefully Tony's message will stick with everyone and will propel us to the winner's platform at the Olympics next year. We now look toward the Olympics. This team will be ready. I will be ready.

Whatever it takes!

Chapter Nineteen

One More
Rocky Road

I found a lot more time to examine my life in the wake of the 1995 World Cup, when I underwent my eleventh knee operation. Recovery time always gives me both reason and opportunity to think.

I realized winning the world championship back in 1991 had been a milestone in my life. In that World Cup I discovered my own capabilities and that I had the talent to be the best in the world. Winning the championship had been a struggle, but I had been rewarded for my efforts with a fantasy moment on the winner's podium, a fairy-tale kind of ending that I now know doesn't always come true.

The 1995 World Cup had been a very different kind of experience—but clearly another milestone. Sweden didn't show me what I could do, but who I was and what

God could do in me. I still hated to lose as much as I ever did. But I found victory despite defeat.

When I found myself knocked out of the '95 World Cup after so much pain and sacrifice to get there, God enabled me to handle the whole horrible experience with grace, dignity, and maturity. I knew I couldn't have done that myself.

Coming to this conclusion marked the point when I really began trusting my life to God. I say that because, before when I was trying to follow God, I hadn't fully, completely, given Him everything. I was still hanging on to soccer—for my own sake, not His. And I also held on to many other areas of my life. Now that I'd learned I could trust God in the very worst of circumstances, I realized I was a lot better off letting Him have complete control.

Of course that was not an easy lesson for me to put into practice every day. Especially when things didn't look like they were going my way.

Like the time during the spring of 1996 when I tore up my knee again and had one doctor tell me I needed an operation that would prevent my playing in the Olympics.

Instead I opted to rehabilitate the knee, which meant two or three hours of physical therapy a day over the next few months trying to get ready. I would come from practice (whether I was watching or participating) in the middle of the day to work my rear end off with Rodney, my physical therapist. Then I'd go back to practice in the afternoon and finally home to collapse in bed.

I would have been a lot more discouraged that spring if I hadn't had some great company to share my misery. My friend Sal (that's the shortened version of Amanda Cromwell's crazy National Women's Team nickname, Sally Mally Wally Jally) blew out her own knee during a training camp scrimmage game.

❂ ❂ ❂

"It meant so much to have someone who I knew understood what I was going through to talk with," Sal says. "We could be honest about our pain and discouragement. In doing that we could encourage each other."

❂ ❂ ❂

I needed that encouragement. The emotional and physical roller-coaster ride with CFIDS continued through the spring.

Some days I cried in the shower and prayed, "Lord, I can't make it through this day. Please give me the strength because I just can't do it."

During that time I picked up a rather controversial book about CFIDS titled *Osler's Web*. What I read really scared me. No one knew the risk of a person with CFIDS trying to compete physically at my level. I could be permanently damaging my body. How much risk was too much?

For the first time, I seriously considered the idea that I might need to give up the game I loved after the Olympics. And I wondered, *What would God want me to do?*

Colleen Hacker, our team psychologist, told me, "God can't direct your steps unless you're taking some." So I decided to start by trying to E-mail Dr. Paul Cheney, a world-renowned specialist in the treatment of CFIDS, to ask his advice. To my surprise, he responded immediately. We set up a phone consultation the next week. When we talked, he did express real concern that I might be risking my ongoing health. He told me I had two choices to reduce that risk—quit playing soccer or try a ten-week Elimination Diet.

That would mean cutting dairy, caffeine, red meat, gluten, and sugar out of my diet. In other words, I could forget anything that tasted good. No more TCBY, no Cinnabons, pizza, or my beloved Starbucks coffee.

I opted for the diet. And since the last day of the tenth week would fall on July 21—the day of our first game in the Olympics—I took that as an encouraging sign. And I began living on gluten-free cereal, Powerbars, dried gluten-free soups, gluten-free bread, rice milk, popcorn, gluten-free pancake mix, corn or rice pastas, peanut butter, and carrots . . . lots of them. I juiced more than two pounds of carrots a day.

My new diet worked wonders. I had increased energy and stamina, balance, peripheral vision, and strength. I was feeling healthier by the week. Then the month before the Olympics, I suffered a grade-two sprain of the joint that attaches the big toe to the foot. It swelled up like a balloon. I couldn't walk on it, let alone run or kick a soccer ball. In fact, I couldn't even wear a shoe on that foot for almost two weeks.

When I was able to practice again, my injured toe had to be carefully taped. But I wasn't about to let a little pain stop me. After everything else I'd been through, I couldn't imagine announcing to the team that I wouldn't be able to play in the Olympics because of an injured toe.

Chapter Twenty

Going for Gold

On July 18 the team traveled by chartered bus from their training center in Sanford, Florida, to the Olympic village at Michelle's alma mater, the University of Central Florida, escorted by motorcycle cops and police cruisers with sirens wailing and lights flashing. Traffic parted like the Red Sea. The city of Orlando, an Olympic venue for soccer only, had adopted the U.S. Women's National Team as their own.

Michelle's teammates then flew to Atlanta for the Opening Ceremonies. She decided to stay behind, afraid the travel and the late night would zap the energy she needed for the tournament. She tried to stay up and watch her friends march in wearing their snazzy red, white, and blue garb, but she fell asleep by 10 p.m.

✥ ✥ ✥

When we marched into the Citrus Bowl for our opening game against Denmark, 25,303 people screamed and cheered and waved flags and banners. That was sixteen thousand more than the largest American crowd to have ever seen us play before. I spotted my dad in the stands and gave him and the rest of my family—Sue, my brother Mike, my mom, my Aunt Gini, my grandparents—my usual thumbs-up and a wave. I had to choke back tears because it meant so much for all of us to be there together as a family. *Pretty doggone cool*, I thought.

The crowd was not only huge but enthusiastic. The Citrus Bowl rocked. Add to all that the Olympic theme and the national anthem . . . and Whoa! We're talking goose bumps and a major lump in the throat. Then the game started and it was all business.

We may have been too keyed up at the start. A number of early shots sailed high. But we steadily wore the Danes down in the 102-degree heat. With 10 minutes to go in the first half, Tish Venturini scored the first Olympic goal in the history of U.S. women's team. Five minutes later I saw another chance.

✥ ✥ ✥

As Denmark got set for their goal kick Michelle told Mia Hamm if the ball came anywhere near her, she was going to head it as hard as she could toward the Denmark goal. "She kept telling me, 'Mia, pinch in,'" Hamm remembers, "because I was too wide. As soon as I moved in, she headed it back in and I had a clear path to the goal. If she hadn't told me to move, I never would have scored that goal." Mia, who had learned to trust Michelle over the years, gave the U.S. a 2–0 lead.

☻ ☻ ☻

We ended up beating Denmark easily by a 3–0 score.

As I'd learned more about CFIDS in recent months I'd started talking to Doc Adams more about the disease and how I was feeling. He did some research on his own and helped come up with a new strategy he thought might help me recover faster after games. He wanted to try IVs to help restore my body fluids and raise my blood pressure faster.

I needed to recover as quickly as possible because we had our second game just two days later. Game two was also a scorching day. We scored early on another beautiful goal by Tish Venturini. But the Swedes fought hard—grabbing arms, shirts, shorts, necks, and anything else they could, to slow down our faster players. The official called them for eighteen fouls, and still a lot of rough stuff went unchecked.

With 16 minutes remaining in the game, Mac (Shannon MacMillan) scored to give us a 2–0 lead. We held on to win 2–1.

❀ ❀ ❀

Mia Hamm was carried off the field with a badly sprained ankle late in the game. Michelle trudged off the field bruised and battered.

Kristine Lilly remembers walking into the training room after the game, "And there's Michelle with an ice bag on her head, an ice bag on her thigh, two more ice bags on her knee and ankle, her hand and toe all taped, hooked up to an IV. I took her picture. She just looked at me and we both burst out laughing."

❀ ❀ ❀

The 0–0 tie against China didn't matter. We both advanced to the next round where we would have to play our old nemesis—Norway.

I felt like I'd reached the beginning of the end. I could barely shower. My symptoms and weariness grew more severe after every game. I was running out of gas earlier during the matches and finding it harder to recover afterwards. Injuries were taking a toll as well.

My right knee had to be drained the day before the Norway game, the result of more torn cartilage in the China game. My big toe still needed to be taped. My hand was taped because of a sprained thumb and finger. And I had a bad quad bruise from a charley horse suffered in the Sweden game. Our trainer, Patty Marshak, joked that half the U.S. soccer budget was being spent on tape just to hold me together. I laughed, but I was worried. It was going to take everything I had just to finish a game against Norway, let alone be an impact player. And I wanted very badly to do well.

✿ ✿ ✿

More than sixty-four thousand fans showed up at Sanford Stadium on the University of Georgia campus to see that semifinal match between the United States and Norway. And Tony DiCicco could not have been happier about Michelle's performance in her new position as a midfielder.

"She really surprised Norway," he remembers. "They had no answer for her. She won every headball that came near her."

Michelle's dominance in the air robbed Norway of their main offensive weapon, long accurate passes from their backs to their front-runners. Virtually every pass Norway flew in her direction went off Michelle's head back toward Norway's goal. They couldn't get their offense started.

✿ ✿ ✿

Not quite halfway through the first half, Norway intercepted a clearance pass and scored. So we went into the half trailing 1–0.

I stumbled into the locker room and sank to the floor. I told Steve Slain, "I can't keep going. I can't do it. I'm outta gas!"

And he kept telling me, "You will finish! You've got to finish! They need you!"

The second half began much like the first. Lilly pushed up the side time after time to create good shots. But we couldn't get the ball in the net. Time was running out. With just 10 minutes left in the game, and our hopes for an Olympic gold fading fast, the official whistled a Norwegian defender for a handball in her own penalty area.

I was sprinting for the corner when the whistle sounded and didn't realize what had happened at first. I could barely stay on my feet and was just grateful for a chance to stop and catch my breath. But the second I realized we were being award a penalty kick, I wanted it.

I looked at Tony, and he pointed at me. I thought, *Rock on!*

Stepping up to the mark, I took the ball from the official. And I thought, *This is the moment I've been waiting for all my life.* I was calm. I was confident. Very aware of the importance of this kick. *If I miss, we'll probably lose and there will be no gold medal.* I decided to go to the left and drive it so hard that if the keeper did get a hand on the ball, it would take her right into the net. I looked to the right and then focused only on the ball during my approach. I felt no doubt.

The goalkeeper guessed and dove right. The ball went left. And the score was tied 1–1. What an incredible feeling! I leaped high into the air, both arms pumping in delight, again and again. Foudy was the first American to get to me before we were mobbed by the rest of the team.

The celebration was short-lived. But it pumped me full of just enough adrenaline to get me to the end of regulation time. Then I crashed again. Hard.

Walking off the field I told Slainer, "That's it. There's nothing left." No one else heard me because I didn't want them to know how bad it was. Steve practically threw me to the ground, onto my back, and started working on me, shaking my legs, shoving a Powerbar and Gatorade down my throat, and insisting, "You can do this!"

Everyone gathered around Tony for instructions prior to overtime. I lay flat on my back in the middle of the huddle. And as I looked up at my teammates stacking hands above me, I prayed for the strength to hold on another few minutes. Steve pulled me to my feet, smacked me on the butt, and told me to get out there and do it.

In the 10th minute of the first overtime Shannon MacMillan took a perfect pass from Foudy and slotted it. When I saw the ball go in I remember thinking, *We did it!* And then *I did it!* I had lasted the entire game and I didn't know how. Well, I did know how. It was only God's strength that had carried me through. Afterward, Doc Adams confirmed that opinion saying, "I don't know how you did it, Mish. It had to be a miracle. There is no other explanation."

It was all I could do to stagger to the locker room.

Afterwards, Slainer and Doc Adams carried me to the bus and finally into the training room at the UGA dorm, got me comfortable on the training table, and hooked up the IV.

Four days later, August 1, 1996, we played the gold medal match at Sanford Stadium in front of 76,481 people—at the time the largest crowd ever to witness a women's sporting event anywhere in the world. I probably had no business being out there at all. Fifteen minutes into the game I knew I had nothing left. But I didn't want to leave because this was the gold medal game.

I guess I was doing okay because Tony didn't yank me.

❂ ❂ ❂

Michelle was doing better than okay.

As in the Norway game, her assignment against China was to win balls in the midfield and distribute them quickly and accurately. That's just what she did in the 18th minute of the game. Tiffeny Milbrett came up with the ball in a crowd and dropped it back to Michelle who led Kristine Lilly perfectly on the left flank. Lilly took the pass, sprinted to the box, and crossed the ball right in front of the goal to Mia Hamm who volleyed a screamer that hit the keeper's hand and bounced off the left post. And there was Shannon Mac to finish off the rebound. USA 1, China 0.

It wasn't long before China came back to tie. The game remained 1–1 at the half. Again Michelle went through her usual halftime routine, trying to rally for the second half.

❂ ❂ ❂

The truth is, very little even registered on my brain that second half. I could hear Loudy Foudy occasionally above the dull roar from the crowd. But that was it.

I was beginning to dread the prospect of yet another overtime as the game passed the 70-minute mark. Then Mia got the ball on the right sideline, and passed it right between two Chinese defenders to a sprinting Joy Fawcett, who carried the ball all the way to the penalty box. And when the keeper charged, Joy slipped the ball left to Millie who poked it in for a 2–1 lead. The stadium went berserk.

But we still had 18 minutes to play. It seemed like forever before the referee's whistle blew once, twice, and the crowd's roar drowned out the third. The game was over.

And my initial feeling was more relief and gratefulness than anything else. *It's over! Now I can rest!*

Of course there was still the little matter of a gold medal ceremony. The team had to change and go back out to the tunnel to wait for the ceremony to begin. I felt so dazed and dizzy I had to sit down. Mia leaned over and told me, "Just a little longer. You can do it." I wasn't so sure.

But when I walked out into that stadium and realized not one of those 76,481 people had left, it all seemed worth it. I found my family in the crowd and raised both arms in a triumphant salute. And then I climbed onto the medal platform for a moment so many people dream about.

Let me tell you, it's everything you imagine. Almost surreal. Extremely emotional. Tears. Laughter. Disbelief. Joy. All at once. And all very overwhelming. When an official International Olympic Committee hung my gold medal around my neck, my first thought was, *Wow! That's heavy!*

The next day, August 2, I wrote in my journal:

> My thoughts are scattered and disjointed, but the sentiment and unforgettable memories will forever be embedded in my heart. My mind keeps returning to the past few years when I thought I was so alone, so isolated in my struggles and pain.
>
> God is so good. Through it all, He was preparing me for this moment, this experience. He's so faithful. He took it all away, but He gave me back so much more.
>
> I go to bed tonight an Olympic champion.

Chapter Twenty-One
Beyond the Games

After the Olympics I needed time off to heal. And to think about my future. So it wasn't until October 30 and November 1 of 1997 that I rejoined the national team to play against Sweden in my only two soccer games of the entire year. I eased back into more of the routine in 1998, playing in fifteen of the national team's twenty-five-game schedule.

The time away from soccer brought exciting new opportunities. My church sent me to Egypt in 1997 to meet with representatives and leaders of Christian congregations from throughout the Mideast to discuss the potential use of sports ministries as evangelistic and outreach tools.

I also got invited to speak at the Billy Graham Crusade in Tampa. Calm and confident, I stood backstage looking out at the sixty thousand people in Raymond James

Stadium waiting for the guy to push me out to the podium. All of a sudden, it was my turn. I ran out there (yes, literally ran) and began talking.

After months of thinking and preparing, now—in three minutes and twenty seconds—I was done. Then as I high-fived everyone backstage and even got a hug from Billy Graham himself, I couldn't help remembering that vision planted in my mind at my grandparents' church three years before—of me speaking to soccer and church groups about God. The idea had seemed so unimaginable, so terrifying, at the time. *Me? Standing up and talking to people about Jesus? No way!*

Now here I was speaking at a Billy Graham Crusade to sixty thousand people. And flying halfway around the world to talk to churches and other Christian groups about using soccer to open doors for sharing the gospel message.

Who would have thought?

My experience in Egypt and then at the Graham Crusade encouraged an idea I'd been thinking about for a while. In 1998, with the help, support, and prayers of many wonderful friends and volunteers, I actually founded a ministry of my own called Soccer Outreach International. The whole idea behind SOI is to work with other groups, churches, and individuals to help challenge, inspire, and equip people—especially kids—to

● ● ●

163

the
GAME
& the
GLORY

reach their potential and achieve their goals and make a difference in the world. We want to impart character and leadership and faith.

As excited as I was about all these opportunities and their implications for my personal life and ministry after soccer, I came to the conclusion during 1997 and 1998 that my own immediate future included the pursuit of another World Cup with the U.S. Women's National Team. After taking more than a year off, much of '98 was spent just working back into playing shape. But by the time our team began its five-month pre-cup residency camp back in Orlando again in January 1999, I was feeling fitter, stronger, healthier, and readier to play soccer than I had in years.

I was excited by the prospect of Women's World Cup '99. But I also knew from experience that the road to another possible world championship would be a grueling one, filled with unexpected obstacles and marked by memorable milestones.

The first milestone came early—on Saturday, January 30—in a game against Portugal in Fort Lauderdale, Florida. My good buddy Millie (Tiffeny Milbrett) sent a beauty of a corner kick into the box where I turned and launched a left-footed volley past a paralyzed keeper for the one hundredth international goal of my career. Since I was only the fourth soccer player in history to do that, my teammates mobbed me, the crowd gave me a nice standing ovation, and they stopped the game to present me with the ball.

The U.S. vs. World All-Stars game in San Jose, California, in February was another milestone—the first women's soccer game in history to be broadcast live to a worldwide audience. The perfect time and place for me to make a spectacle of myself. It happened as I was leaping for a ball off a corner kick in just the 19th minute of the match. My face collided with the back of my Norwegian buddy Linda Mendalen's head and I went down and out. The emergency room folks sewed up the gash over my left eye with twenty-five stitches, found three broken bones around my eye socket, and diagnosed a concussion.

When I finally looked at myself in the mirror two days later, I couldn't pry my left eyelid open far enough to see daylight. The whole side of my face was purple and swollen and I still couldn't stand up for long without throwing up.

Back in Florida on March 3, I underwent outpatient surgery to have the knot on my cheekbone removed and what's called a *closed reduction,* meaning the doctor pulled the crushed bones out to their normal position without opening me up. Though I still looked like I'd tried to kiss a freight train, the plastic surgeon told me I should heal up as good as new. The doc even cleared me to go to

Portugal with the team to play in the annual Algarve Cup just ten days later.

In spite of feeling so physically fit when the year started, the injuries and the intensity of our training combined with the draining demands of our team's pre–World Cup travel schedule took its usual toll on my health. Instead of gradually building my strength as training is supposed to do, the CFIDS symptoms seemed their worst in May, only a month before the tournament was to begin. I hit what felt like absolute bottom when I pulled myself in the middle of a game against Holland up in Milwaukee, Wisconsin. I went into the locker room, totally discouraged and exhausted from the mental battle and the physical struggle, and bawled like a baby.

I continued to put a positive face on things with the media. And the truth was I felt great about our team's prospects in the tournament because I had such confidence in my teammates. We had eight players on our roster with over one hundred caps (international game appearances) who brought incredible veteran leadership to go with exceptional skills.

My biggest doubts centered on my own ability to play. And not just *to play*, but to contribute.

But I took great comfort in something my pastor said in a sermon about spiritual obedience. He said when God calls us to do something, it is not our place to worry about what's going to happen, or even how we're going to do what He asks us to do. If we're willing to be used, our first priority is to "just show up."

So that was my personal strategy going into the World Cup. I had no idea how well, or even if, I could perform through six grueling games over three intensely competitive weeks. But since I remained convinced that God's plan for my life included one more World Cup tournament, I was going to "just show up."

Then, like everyone else, I'd just have to wait and see what happened after that.

Chapter Twenty-Two
Rock On, USA

Most of you who have read this far probably know what happened in the '99 Women's World Cup. So there is little point in a play-by-play recounting of the entire tournament here.

What I will share is a quick look at some very personal highlights drawn from what I wrote in the heat of the moment during the tournament—on my own web page, in my personal journal, and for ESPN.com which also asked for and posted a tournament diary.

WWC OPENER, JUNE 19, 1999
USA VS. DENMARK, GIANTS STADIUM, METRO, NJ

Walking out of the tunnel is always one of my favorite parts of game day. The walkway to the field is usually lined with security, game officials, staff, and media. As you move past them, you hear words of encouragement, cameras whirling and clicking, and people stick out their hands for high fives as you walk past. Jogging out of the tunnel, the stadium slowly wakes up to our entrance. At first, the clamor and crowd noise is soft. But then, it slowly builds into one big, deafening noise. As the cheering increases, it almost physically lifts me up. It is cool to just stand there and let that sink in.

This crowd, though, was extra special. First, it was the largest crowd for a women's sporting event ever (in the history of the world). And second, it was the largest sporting crowd ever for Giants Stadium. The only bigger event was for the Pope. Not bad for a bunch of girls, huh?

The memories I have of this game are:

- Looking for my dad and friends and not being able to find them.

- How doggone hot it was on the field and how dry my mouth was.

- A jam-packed stadium of swirling banners and signs, and yelling, cheering fans.

- Bri (Brianna Scurry) getting the wind knocked out of her.

- Heading the ball about six thousand times.

- Tackling and tracking like a maniac.

- The ref yelling at me to let her take care of the fouls (meaning don't play extra rough to even things out).

- The goals by Lil, Mia, and Foudy. Wow.

- The final whistle: 3–0.

- The on-field celebration. Yippeeeeeeee.

- Waving and thanking the crowd for being so awesome.

We did it. One down, five more to go.

WWC GAME 2, JUNE 24, 1999
USA VS. NIGERIA, SOLDIER FIELD, CHICAGO

Once the opening whistle blew in this game, we were transformed instantaneously into a bunch of bungling idiots. We stumbled around, gave away the ball, collided with each other, chased frantically, and in general, lost control of our bodily functions and brainpower.

In contrast to our nightmare beginning, the Nigerians came out on fire and scored in the first 2 minutes to put them up 1–0. Thankfully, we have enough veteran seasoning to know a game is a 90-minute ordeal and we had another 88 minutes to rectify the situation. As we dug the ball out of the net, we collectively took a deep breath, and set to the task of getting on the scoreboard. It didn't take long. We immediately rallied to score a bunch of goals (an "own" goal mistake by Nigeria, another blast from Mia, a Tiff Milbrett special, a header from me, and a bunch of others that, as usual, I can't remember for the life of me) which brought us 7–1 victory.

Two games down, four to go. Rock on, USA.

WWC GAME 3, JUNE 27, 1999
USA VS. N. KOREA, FOXBORO STADIUM, BOSTON

This game was dedicated to a church friend of mine from Orlando who is battling cancer and has the most remarkable perspective and attitude toward life. I wrote Laurie's name on my sock tape with the reference Joshua

1:9, a verse which says, "Have I not commanded you? Be strong and courageous. Do not be terrified; do not be discouraged, for the LORD your God will be with you wherever you go."

Laurie gave me this verse the day before I left for WC and I have not forgotten her slant on what God is saying to her (and me) through this incredible command and promise. Here's what I took into the game:

1. Being strong and courageous is not optional. God demands courageous living from me and will not tolerate me wimping out because I am chicken.

2. God is my strength and courage and is with me wherever I go. Rock on. The point of this is I don't find strength or courage through my own resources (i.e., my knowledge, willpower, abilities, etc.), but I choose it because I know God is beside me—always. He becomes my strength, my confidence, my courage; and with Him at my side, I can overcome CFIDS, accept defeat or disappointment, fall in love, win a world championship, walk into an uncertain future, or face any circumstance with absolute confidence and boldness.

Knowing this promise and having this perspective gives me extraordinary freedom to really go for it in my life and on the soccer field.

Tony and staff put out a different lineup against the North Koreans. The strategy for this game was to win (of course), but also to rest and protect various players for the quarterfinal vs. Germany. So I got stuck on the bench for the entire match.

At the end of the 3–0 game, the team did the usual victory lap to acknowledge the crowd. This is always a fun time because everyone goes nuts as you run past, and we get the opportunity to say thanks for being such stud fans. Well, I was running along the field by the stadium wall high-fiving people, totally enjoying the moment, when some dude grabbed my arm and jerked me off my feet. I landed on the pavement and when I tried to catch myself, my shoulder gave way. I immediately knew I had sublexed it (meaning it went out and quickly back in the socket).

I don't know who did this and I assume he didn't mean to hurt me. He probably thought it would be funny to grab me and was just being playful, but now I have to deal with an injured shoulder on top of everything else. Thankfully, I should be good to go on Thursday vs. Germany, but the fact I (we) have to deal with this at all is crazy. So, fans, if I don't get too close, please understand. It only takes one goofball to ruin a perfectly fun and innocent exchange. And unfortunately, I am running out of body parts.

Great game, good win, and super fans. Three down, and three to go.

Chapter Twenty-Three

Time to Cowboy Up

Two more of my personal World Cup diary reports:

Wooooooooooooo weeeeeeeeeeeeeeeee. What a game. My heart is just now recovering from the drama and craziness of this one.

We expected the Germans to be tough. They always are. But knowing that (in our brains) and experiencing it (alive and down our throats) are two different things. Much of our team seemed flat for the kickoff and suddenly, off a mistake backpass to Bri, we are down one to a very good German team. We rallied a tying goal (by Millie) soon after, but German midfielder number 10 stuck a beautiful one in to put them up again 2–1 at the end of the first half. My body already felt 90-minute exhausted from the (defensive) workload of the first half. But somehow I managed to find an inner reservoir that I hoped would be enough to carry me another 45 minutes.

Time to cowboy up (as the rodeo dudes say). And cowboy up we did.

The second half was a whole new game for us. Our focus sharpened, our mentality hardened, and we fought tooth and nail to overcome our deficit. Brandi tied the game off a loose ball in the box. Then, Joy connected with Mac (a sweet header off a corner) to put us ahead by one goal. The last minutes of the game were agonizing.

The one thought that ran unceasingly through my head was, *Do not let them score, do not let them score, do not let them score, do not let them score.* I was so fearful of a freak goal in the last minutes of the game, all I could think of was to boot the ball (and the opponent if necessary) as far down the field or out of the stadium as possible.

Our postgame celebration was very emotional this time. We gathered in the middle of the field and exchanged some heartfelt, intense words before waving and acknowledging the crowd. When I found my dad on the other side of the stadium, I jumped the signage, climbed the stairs into the stands, and gave him a big hug. I dedicated this game to him and had written POPS on my sock tape. When I showed him, he cried. It was a neat moment.

I sure do love my Pops.

Now we face Brazil for the semifinal on Sunday.

Once again, time to cowboy up.

WWC SEMIFINAL, JULY 4, 1999
USA VS. BRAZIL, STANFORD STADIUM, PALO ALTO, CA

We won!!! 2–0. Yippeeeeeeee. We are through to the final. Another frantic, frenzied game for us, but we managed to pull it out with an awesome performance from Bri and an incredible defensive effort from the team as a whole. Bri made three incredible saves and got MVP of the game. She rocked big time. CP (Cindy Parlow) got the first goal off a mishandled ball by the keeper (in the first 5 minutes) and in the 80th minute Mia got taken down and I scored the PK. Whew. I celebrated exactly like I did in the Olympics (jumping up and down).

This game was a rough one for me. I got my bell rung (head-to-head collision) and have a big knot on the back of my head; and if that wasn't enough, I also got a cleat to the face (courtesy of Sissi). Thankfully, I got my arm up before she got me and that took the brunt of it or it could have been bad news. As it is, I have a cleat mark on the bridge of my nose and a bruise/welt above my eye. And yes, it is the same eye/side of my face that got busted up before. Thank God I don't have to go through that again.

Brazil played their usual game of flair and dangerous one-on-one stuff. But we played tough and disciplined defense for the entire 90 minutes. I tell you what, defense is much harder than attacking. The effort, focus, discipline, vision, and intensity required is enormous. Not only do you have to physically be in the game, and ready to rock at any given moment, but the mentality and concentration must be laser-like as well. There is absolutely no room for error. One lapse and the player is open and the ball is in the back of the net.

So, now we go into the final vs. China.

Five down, one to go.

✪ ✪ ✪

Actually it's six games plus two overtimes down, and now one shoot-out to go. We're back at the World Cup final on July 10 in the Rose Bowl, where we started at the first of this book. When I said it wasn't the end of my story...

Chapter Twenty-Four
My Cup Runneth Over

Even after 90 minutes of scoreless regulation time and two scoreless overtimes the World Cup final is not yet final. It's China 0, USA 0. I am lying on that training table in the medical triage room, down in the gray bowels of that historic old stadium, when Doc Adams tells me we are going to a penalty kick shoot-out.

I don't remember actually watching the first nine kicks. After receiving two liters of IV fluids I was only starting to plug back in mentally. I couldn't see the television screen while lying on my back on the training table. I couldn't even tell for sure what was happening by the reactions of the medical team, as they huddled around the television groaning when China made one and cheering when the U.S. scored.

You wouldn't believe the screaming and celebrating that took place in that examination room when Liu Ying sent her shot toward the goal, only to have Brianna Scurry step up, guess left, dive that way, and deflect the ball wide of the net. When Kristine Lilly converted her kick we suddenly had a very real advantage—three goals to two.

After Zhang Ouying, Mia Hamm, and, of course, Sun Wen all made their shots, the score was tied 4–4, with one last American turn to come. I remember Doc Adams somehow propped me in a sitting position so I could see the TV screen for Brandi Chastain's kick. The moment her left-footed blast rocketed past a late-diving Gao Hong and smacked the back of the net, I saw Doc almost jump through the ceiling. But not until he ran over, got right in my face, and started yelling, "We won! We won!" did the reality finally begin to sink in.

I slumped down and started crying in relief.

Then I said, "Get this stuff out of me!" (meaning the IV). "I'm going out there!"

Someone handed me an official yellow World Champion T-shirt to replace the game jersey that had been cut off. Doc helped me off the table and then walked me slowly out the locker room door for the now-familiar jaunt through the passageways winding under the stadium. I reached the tunnel leading out to the field, only to find a very large and imposing man in a blue police uniform blocking my way. "I'm not supposed to allow anyone out on the field," he told me.

Since I was wearing a yellow T-shirt instead of my game jersey I guess he didn't realize I was a team member. "But I'm a player...."

"They said 'No one!'"

I tried to step past him. He easily moved in front of me.

I can't believe this! I thought. *My team has just won the 1999 World Cup. My teammates are celebrating and receiving their championship medals this very moment. And I can't walk out on the field to join them.* I was so frustrated and fatigued I didn't know whether I was going to cry or pass out.

Just then, behind the policeman, someone with official credentials recognized me. When they said, "Let her through!" the cop immediately stepped back. The next thing I knew Doc Adams took me by the arm to steady me as we traipsed down the tunnel and out onto the end zone grass.

I could barely make out the awards platform through the blizzard of shredded paper spewing from confetti cannons positioned all around the stadium. It wasn't until I'd begun shuffling across the field on a thick blanket of torn paper and felt the confetti sticking to the bottom of my bare feet that I realized I'd come out without any shoes or socks on.

In the time it took Doc and me to make a slow tiring journey to midfield, the official awards ceremony ended.

The crowd roared as my victorious teammates stood on the podium waving their thanks to our fans. That was still going on when Doc helped me up the steps at the end of the platform. FIFA president Sepp Blatter recognized me in the maelstrom. Walking quickly toward me, he draped a leftover medal around my neck, hugged me, and congratulated me while kissing me on both cheeks in formal European style.

As my teammates realized my presence, there was a huge round of hugs with more than enough shared tears to soak much of my new yellow T-shirt. By the time I'd hugged everyone I was getting wobbly. I needed a place to rest. Immediately.

"Over here, Mish," Doc Adams said as he eased me back down to the field—until I was half leaning, half sitting against the edge of the awards platform. While the team took a victory lap I was content to sit there alone in all that happy, milling madness, soaking in the continuing roar of the crowd and watching as my teammates raced frantically around the field, greeting well-wishers, waving to family and friends in the stands, and repeatedly hugging one another.

Suddenly Sal walked up and gave me a big hug. She'd been in the stands watching the game. "How'd you get out here, Sal?" I exclaimed in surprise, remembering the big policeman. Then I cried some more over the unexpected chance to share this moment with a friend who knew, perhaps better than anyone else in the world, what this moment meant to me. And for what I knew it meant to Sal after her 1996 knee injury had ended her national team career and shattered her own longtime dream of playing in this World Cup.

Sal grinned through her own happy tears. "You hear that, Mish?"

"Hear what?"

"The crowd!"

I tried to tune in the noise. "What do you mean?"

"Listen. They're calling your name, Mish."

Finally I heard it too. From around the stadium. In a rising chant. "Aaa-kers! Aaa-kers! Aaa-kers!" It quickly spread and grew louder. "Aaa-kers! Aaa-kers! Aaa-kers!"

Tears started streaming down my face.

"Mish, you gotta acknowledge 'em," Sal said. "Go on."

"C'mon. Go with me." I wanted to share the moment with her. So Sal helped me to my feet and ushered me from the side of the awards platform and slowly out toward the very middle of the field.

The applause and the cheers grew louder. I trudged a little oblong loop, maybe ten yards across at the widest point. And as people continued to call "Aaa-kers! Aaa-kers! Aaa-kers!" I faced all four corners of the Rose Bowl, pointing and clapping and waving back at a world record crowd I couldn't actually see through my tears.

I stood there until I thought I'd keel over. Then Sal, who'd walked close behind to make sure I was all right, caught up and helped me off the field after what may have been the shortest victory lap in history.

"Let's get you back inside," Doc Adams suggested. I didn't resist as he and Sal led me slowly toward the tunnel.

The locker room celebration was well under way by the time I finally got there. Cheers and laughter filled the air. Doc and Sal ushered me through a crush of media, teammates, and soccer officials—to the back of the locker room. Doc helped me lie down right on the cool concrete floor and started yet another IV. "If you don't get your act together soon, Mish," he warned me, "we're going to have to take you to the ER."

A long time passed before most of the outsiders finally drifted out of the locker room, and things grew gradually quieter. By then, the added fluids had begun to clear my head enough that I could come out for a quick meeting with just my teammates. A private time where the staff and Tony thanked and congratulated us all.

Looking around that locker room full of totally exhausted faces and ear-to-ear smiles, I knew we were sharing a moment and a feeling none of us would ever forget. *World Champions again! Incredible!*

The meeting over, Doc Adams hooked me up to the IV once more. And there, lying on my back again in that victorious locker room, with the fourth and final liter of IV fluid running into my arm, I could finally think. I realized that as excited as I was to have achieved our team goal and won the 1999 World Cup, I felt an even greater sense of personal satisfaction knowing that I'd been faithful and given my all. And I knew even then that, for me, the most lasting and powerfully meaningful memory of the entire day would be the incredible gift I'd received from the Rose Bowl crowd when they'd chanted my name.

I could still hear the echo in my mind. *Aaa-kers! Aaa-kers! Aaa-kers!* What a tribute! It was as if they'd seen my heart.

Epilogue

I t's amazing to see what God can do when we just show up.

The aftermath of the World Cup has been absolutely mind-boggling for the Women's National Team, and for me personally. Because of the wear and tear of the tournament and previously made commitments, I turned down a zillion media opportunities and was unable to do all the appearances with my team, including the obligatory visit to the White House. I needed time to recover.

Since the World Cup, my most important commitment has been cheering on someone who has cheered me on more than a million times: my Pops. Just weeks after our victory, he had a cancerous tumor removed from his colon, and as I write today, he is facing aggressive chemotherapy with a good prognosis. Watching him struggle through this is heart wrenching. I hate it. Now I know what it's like when he helplessly sees me battle CFIDS and injuries. I'm also reminded again where I got a large measure of my own grit and guts.

Wheaties made me the first soccer player ever to appear on a box of "The Breakfast of Champions." I agreed to author this book and a second one about my life written for adults to read. A number of companies wanted to talk about endorsement deals. I continue to have to screen all these opportunities in order to conserve my energy and maintain my focus on those things that really matter. Faith. Family. Friends. And whatever God has in store for my future.

As of now I intend to show up at the 2000 Olympics in Australia and see what happens there. After that? We'll see.

I do know that God has bigger and better plans for my life than I could ever dream of. Soccer Outreach International is already working with other groups and churches to conduct outreach events in Australia around the Olympics—using the same model we used at World Cup venues around the U.S. during the 1999 tournament. After I retire I expect to expand my involvement with SOI, working with kids, and spreading the great game of soccer and an even greater message of faith and hope around the world.

I also know this. I have played and lived one way my whole life. Full speed ahead, on my own terms, in my own strength, and brushing aside any hint of personal heartache, fear, or frailty. Looking back, it is easy to see why that approach was destined to leave me alone, empty, and without hope.

I now know there is a better way. God's way. And I want to help other people learn some of the lessons I've learned the hard way.

That when we're discouraged and think no one understands us, we can be certain that God knows and loves each one of us individually. We are God's kids. He knows who we are, He hears our innermost thoughts, and still loves us completely and perfectly.

That when we feel worthless or just don't know what to do next, we can know that God created each of us for a specific purpose and wants to help us reach our potential. He gives each of us special and unique gifts, talents, looks, strengths, and so forth—everything we need to become who we are created to be. And His great plan for our lives can be a wonderful adventure if we're willing to find and follow it.

But most of all I want to let people know the most important lesson I've learned. That no matter how tough, or talented, or successful I think I am, I can't make it through life by myself. I need God's help and strength. Friends and family may also disappoint me at times. But I now know that no matter what I have to face in the days and years ahead, I can trust Him. He will always be with me.

I've got a new game plan now. On and off the field, I want to play, work, and live for His glory.